HomeBuilding
PITFALLS

Lawrence Thomas

with Robert Batcheller

New Community Press • Cincinnati, Ohio

HomeBuilding Pitfalls

Insider's guide to getting the quality new home you deserve!
Lawrence Thomas
with Robert Batcheller

www.HomeBuildingPitfalls.com

Published by:
New Community Press
2692 Madison Road N-1 #263
Cincinnati, Ohio 45208
e-mail: NewCommunityPress@cinci.rr.com

Author Inquiries:
HomeBuilding Pitfalls
Post Office Box 8218
Cincinnati, Ohio 45208
e-mail: Lawrence@HomeBuildingPitfalls.com
Toll free: (888) 578-0766

This book is designed to provide general information on the process of buying a newly built house. It is sold with the understanding that neither the publisher nor the authors are engaged in rendering architectural, engineering, or legal advice. The authors recommend that new home buyers seek the advice and guidance of legal and building professionals to assist them in the construction and purchase of a new home.

© Copyright 2003, Lawrence Thomas
Revised Second Printing
ISBN, print edition: 0-9719550-9-3
Library of Congress Control Number: 2002110221

About the guide

This guide is the culmination of knowledge of several attorneys, architects, mortgage lenders, and home builders. Until recently, the main author worked for one of the largest builders in the country.

The original idea for the guide came from one of the authors who left the homebuilding industry because of the terrible changes he began to see. He was disheartened that the rapid growth in new home sales came at the expense of quality construction and customer satisfaction.

In the last ten years, relatively small homebuilding companies have grown and merged into giants. Today, roughly 70% of new homes in this country are built by only 7% of the builders (November 2001, Journal of Light Construction). These "production" builders have enjoyed immense prosperity in this boom-time but have had to deal with a shrinking labor pool of qualified contractors.

Strong demand for new homes, mergers in the industry, and a shrinking qualified labor pool have had disastrous results.

Of the 100 or so *MAJOR* residential building failures (those requiring more than $50,000 to remedy) the authors worked on in the years 2000 and 2001, most were houses that were less than three years old.

The declining quality in recent years is only one factor in the overall dissatisfaction of new home buyers. When talking to new home buyers, the authors often hear complaints about not only the quality of their new home, but the whirlwind homebuilding process they were just forced to endure.

The authors came to realize that many of the problems customers were having could have been prevented. If they had only been aware of the pitfalls they would face, they could have taken action to protect themselves and make the homebuilding experience more enjoyable. The problem was that there was no way for the customer to gain the insider information that they needed about the home-building process. That is what this guide will uncover for you.

Contents

The Foundation: Setting Expectations to Reality

The ideal homebuilding experience would follow this scenario: An informed buyer would choose a trusted, well-established home builder. The builder would employ a competent construction supervisor who would effectively schedule qualified subcontractors to perform the construction work. An honest and knowledgeable inspector would verify the quality of the home. The new homeowners would then move into their new home and enjoy it for years to come. Unfortunately, this is not always the case.

More often than not, most people begin their search for a new home with a trip to a model home or a visit to a large community of new homes. However, behind most beautiful model homes and master-planned communities you will often find companies applying an assembly-line attitude to new home construction instead of the care and craftsmanship advertised to home buyers. By the end of the building process, some buyers find themselves angry and upset after enduring lies, disrespect, poor quality, and bad service.

Larger builders increasingly dominate the homebuilding landscape across this country. The larger builders use standardized plans and construct anywhere from one hundred to tens of thousands of homes a year. These homes can range in price from $100,000 to well over $500,000. In most big cities, large builders create expansive "master planned" communities with amenities such as swimming pools, tennis courts, and play areas. If you are an average home buyer, you will be purchasing a home with a price tag of just over $200,000. And what are you getting for hundreds of thousands of dollars? Craftsmanship? Fine materials? Impeccable service? Unfortunately, far too often the answer is "no."

Frequently, customers' expectations are not in line with the realities of today's big industry of homebuilding. All too often, when people decide to buy a newly built home, they are unaware of how involved they will need to become in the experience.

I should know. From my college days as a co-op student working for a growing home builder, to more recently literally reconstructing poorly constructed homes for a large, luxury builder, I have seen the best and the worst the industry has to offer.

I have watched excited families move into their first new home and realize "The American Dream." I have also watched builders turn their backs on customers who have just made the biggest purchase of their lives. I have witnessed builders pack up and abandon a city, leaving homeowners holding the bag and wondering who will honor the promises made to them of a beautiful new home for their family.

The good news is that that by picking up this book, you have taken the first step in making your new home experience a pleasant one.

When Reality Hits...

Constructing even one home can be a difficult endeavor. Constructing hundreds or thousands of homes in several cities, states, or even countries (as some of the largest builders in the country do) takes a great deal of expertise. Huge regulatory battles complicate purchasing and developing land. Labor and material shortages change timelines. Builders risk major financial investments before the first home is even sold.

Building a home is an imperfect process. Things almost NEVER go EXACTLY as planned. If you walked into any of your neighbors' homes, into your home builder's model home, or into a similar home in another area of town and you really took the time to look closely in all the nooks and crannies, you would find some of the same types of minor imperfections that your new home will have. In reality, people rarely notice such imperfections unless they really look for them. Besides, you can teach yourself the finer points of drywall repair, painting, and caulking in a weekend. However, you don't want to find yourself caught in an expensive legal battle over a major defect in your home such as a structural problem right beneath your feet that could compromise not just the home's resale value, but also the health and safety of your family.

You will likely find legitimate mistakes or flaws that will need to be addressed during the production of your home. My goal for this book is to help you focus your energy on the biggest, most difficult to correct steps in the building process and to help you avoid getting bogged down with small battles and losing sight of the big picture.

As you will read in this book, "new home" does not mean "trouble-free home." I do not recommend buying a new house solely because you are "not handy." Like a new car, your new home will require maintenance and some understanding on your part as to how it works. Even more important than understanding how your house works is understanding the homebuilding process and each of the players in the game.

My goal is to keep you focused on the big picture throughout the entire homebuilding process. That process starts much earlier than the turn of the first shovel of dirt and continues long past your move-in date. I will show you how to protect yourself before you even step foot inside a model home all the way through to having warranty service performed on your new house.

This book follows the order of the homebuilding process. Along the way I will lend an "insider's" view of the homebuilding industry through "Industry Insights." Each chapter contains "Web Icons" denoted by the ♦**WWW**♦ symbol to provide topical links to the World Wide Web if you need more information on any of the points covered. The links can be found on our site:

www.homebuildingpitfalls.com/updatedbooklinks.html

The construction chapter offers a great overview of the entire construction process. However, this is a guide to **having a new home built for you**, not a guide on **how to build a home**. Because there are so many people involved in the process of building a home, I have come to realize that it is more important to understand their roles in the process than it is to completely understand the interrelationship of every component of a house. I will explain the roles of each player in the new home game and how each should perform to ensure that you get the best house for your money. I will share with you the pitfalls of the hundreds of homeowners I have dealt with so that you won't have to repeat the agony that so many new-home buyers have endured.

HomeBuilding
PITFALLS

Chapter One:

Researching the Community

If you already live in the general area of where you are going to build your new home, this section may not be as relevant as others for you. If, however, you are transferring due to a job or relocating for other reasons, it is critical that you understand the community where you will be building. First, gather some general community information.

A) What are the public schools like? ♦WWW♦
You may not think this is important if you either do not intend to send your children to public schools or don't have children, but

the performance of a school district where a residential property is located is one of the key factors in estimating or appraising its value. Even if you don't have kids, your school district is an important factor in the resale price of your new home.

To evaluate the public schools in your area, you should ask:

- *How do the students perform on standardized tests?* This information can be found from a number of sources. The first and easiest place to look is on the Web. Most school districts and individual schools publish their performance statistics on a home page. If they don't have a Web presence, or don't publish these statistics, you should be leery!

- *What are the student-to-teacher ratios?* Smaller class sizes mean more attention for individual students. In fast-growing areas (especially in large metropolitan areas) small class sizes are indicative of well-managed growth.

- *Is the district keeping up with growth?* You can quickly figure this out by looking at total class size by grade. If you see a large concentration of kids at certain grade levels and no plans for new facilities for these students as they matriculate, a problem may exist. If you live in a fast-growing community now, you know what I am talking about. All too often, the following occurs:

  1. An area becomes desirable partly because of the quality of the school system.
  2. A rise in new home construction follows, bringing in new families looking to take advantage of the quality school system.
  3. An increased number of students overwhelm a system caught without a plan to manage growth.

4. Classes become overcrowded and facilities overwhelmed.
5. The quality of education decreases.

When I worked in land development for a large builder, we would market either the overall quality of the school system (district) or try to sell the proximity of the schools. For some reason, a new elementary school that was close by but in a less desirable school district was just as easy to sell as a great overall school district.

B) How do city services rate? ♦WWW♦

Think about all of the services that a good municipality may provide: police and fire protection, trash pick-up, recreation areas, and libraries. Does your target community provide these services? Should they be doing so (considering the amount of taxes you will be paying)? Do not assume that all communities provide all services. Services such as curbside recycling, yard waste disposal, and snow removal on side streets may seem basic, but not every community offers them.

And don't forget about:
- proximity of hospitals, shopping, dining, places of worship
- rush-hour traffic
- crime rate

C) What about Taxes?

Don't make the mistake of investigating only property taxes in the area in which you plan to live. A number of taxes of which you may not be aware (especially if you are moving from one state to another) include:

- sales tax
- use tax

- personal property tax
- income tax (state and local- see below)
- inheritance tax

A property may also fall in special tax areas such as fire protection districts, public school systems, public library systems, solid waste districts, cities, townships, and other special taxing districts that may affect the real property tax rate. Remember to factor in tax calculation methods when you compare property tax rates. Some municipalities only tax your property based on a portion of its assessed value. For example, if the property tax rate was 3 percent on a property with an assessed value of $100,000, the tax would be $3,000 per year. But if the municipality only taxes *half* the assessed value, your *effective* tax rate would also be half or 1.5 percent. And don't forget the dreaded income tax. Some municipalities charge you a tax on any income earned within the city's limit. Be sure to check with the city or county auditor or property assessor for your community's specific tax requirements.

D) SAF – Special Assessment Financing
Typically, developers are responsible for installing the infrastructure (streets, sewer lines, etc.) for a neighborhood. At the completion of the project, the developer turns over the ownership of the infrastructure to the applicable city or county government. Because a developer benefits from the sale of lots, he must finance the infrastructure. However, situations exist where property owners pay for the infrastructure through Special Assessment Financing (SAF). With SAF, the infrastructure is financed through bonds issued by the municipality and paid off through a special assessment or tax on the property owners. In this type of arrangement, the developer is usually creating something of benefit to the area, besides new homes, such as a park or golf course that will benefit all residents of the city, not just the new homeowners.

HomeBuilding
PITFALLS

Chapter Two:

Production Homebuilding

If you are in the market for a new home and you find yourself going from model home to model home, you are considered a "production home" buyer. If you have a unique house plan that you would like to have built, you are viewed as a "custom home" buyer. This book focuses on the "big builders" or "production builders" that are responsible for such a large portion of all new homes built in the U.S. ♦**WWW**♦

Production Builders and the Stationary Assembly Line

You will almost never hear builders refer to themselves as "production builders." Production builders don't want you to think of your home as coming off of an assembly line. Builders want you to think of your home as uniquely yours -- even if most of the people in your neighborhood live in the same model, type, or floor plan. But even between two similar models, there can be tens, even hundreds of thousands of dollars in sales price difference due to options and upgrades. The same is true for automobiles. Many vehicles are built on the same platform but vary widely in price. For example, while Toyota and Lexus share platforms and components, they differ by options and finish. Production home builders are no different. If you have essentially the same floor plan (platform) as your neighbor, it is likely that your home was assembled using many of the same components as your neighbor's home. However, we know that homes don't move down a production line with workers assembling components. Instead, homes are stationary and the workers move from home to home repeating similar tasks on similar homes.

Unfortunately, builders haven't figured out a way to build the end product (the house) with the consistent quality of a Toyota or Lexus. To a production builder's credit, coordinating the construction of hundreds, even thousands of homes simultaneously across the country requires a well-thought-out process and a great number of resources.

The process of building thousands of homes involves the coordination of land acquisition and development, product design, marketing, subcontractor scheduling, and supervision. All of this must come together in diverse markets with different regulations, labor demands, market needs, and risk.

The biggest builders have enormous financial resources, buying power, and clout with subcontractors. They usually have long-established relationships with banks that allow them to weather downturns in the market. Because of the number of homes they construct, big production builders get the best prices on materials from lumber to carpet. Many subcontractors rely on the steady stream of work that production builders provide.

While big builders are good at certain things, they are not good at change. They don't like to change wording on their contracts, customize a home plan, or leave anything to chance. They want the process to be like that of buying a car-- you go into the showroom (model home), choose your model and color (selections), and make your purchase (they get their money at closing). Unfortunately, the homebuilding process is not that easy.

For the remainder of this book I will use the term "large builder" or "builder" to refer to a production builder. There is no such thing as a large "custom builder." It would be extremely difficult to build thousands of purely "custom" homes a year the way production builders build thousands of similar homes a year. There is, however, such thing as a small production builder. A builder constructing only fifty houses a year can employ production builder techniques by limiting their portfolio of homes to just a few and borrowing construction techniques from larger production builders.

www.HOMEBUILDINGPITFALLS.com

HomeBuilding
PITFALLS

Chapter Three:

Researching Your Builder

Since building a home is an average family's largest investment, it is important to look further than the model home or sales rep for information on the builder. You should not blindly trust the builder's propaganda, (marketing literature and claims of 100 percent customer satisfaction). As an example, I know of a builder that had a unique way of claiming 100 percent customer satisfaction. The company had a policy that no home would close with incomplete and outstanding items on the "punch list" (a list used to document unfinished work). While that is a good policy, by signing a form that stated that all items were complete, the home buyer agreed they were 100 percent satisfied with the home. The twisted logic found that if you closed, you were 100 percent satisfied with your home, and therefore the company had "100 percent customer satisfaction." The reality was that more than a few unsatisfied customers were forced to sign off on uncompleted items because they had a moving truck on the way.

What is the Builder's Reputation in the Community?
Unless the company is newly formed or very small, this information should not be hard to find, especially with the assistance of the Internet. Third-party information (not supplied by the builder) is available in online versions of most large newspapers and business journals.

Online business journals are great sources for local business news, including important reports on the financial stability of builders. Searching the archives of journals listed in www.bizjournals.com offers insights into builders' projects and problems. Bizjournals.com offers business news for some of the fastest-growing housing markets including Atlanta, Dallas, Houston, South Florida, and San Francisco. Searching is simple… just put the name of the builder in the search engine and see what results appear. Another search technique is to perform a search on the Web site of the major newspaper where your builder is based. Finally, don't forget to drop your builder's name into a search engine like Yahoo! or Google. ◆**WWW**◆

Keep in mind, the larger the builder, the greater the chance you will find complaints about the builder. Entering "Pulte problems" into a search engine will produce some interesting sites. As one of the largest home builders in North America, Pulte has disgruntled homeowners that use the Web as one of their tools to make people aware of their problems.

Industry Insight: *Biting the Hand That Feeds You*:
You are less likely to find damning reports and exposés on specific builders in major metropolitan newspapers because builders are some of the largest purchasers of ad space in newspapers. Just pick up a major newspaper's weekend real estate section and look at the full-page ads. Those advertisements cost tens of thousands of dollars each week. Some newspapers would think twice about sacrificing a strong ad revenue stream by reporting on a local builder's problem.

One constant in the homebuilding process is that homeowners are always willing to talk about their new homes and their experiences with their builder. Take a walk through the neighborhood where you are looking to buy and strike up a conversation with a few of your potential neighbors. Besides getting an education on the builder you can also get to know some of the people in the neighborhood.

Ask them specifics:
- Did they choose the right lot?
- Did they make any mistakes in their selection process?
- How often did they visit the building site during construction?
- What was their experience in dealing with their builder?
- What problems are common with this builder?
- How responsive is the builder to their problems?
- Would they build again with this builder?

Once you talk with a few homeowners, you should get a feel for the strengths and weaknesses of the builder and the community.

For smaller builders, don't be shy about asking for the names and numbers of a few customers. Call them up and ask them about their experiences.

Industry Insight: *Let the Truth Not Be Known!*
Time has shown that walking the neighborhood and talking to a builder's customers is the best way to get the "skinny" on a builder. However, don't believe everything you hear. While visiting a homeowner about a serious warranty issue (read about this serious mold problem in Appendix A: Moisture Problems), a common complaint arose: "But nobody ever told us." When I usually heard such a complaint, it was from a homeowner upset that the builder did not disclose a problem to the customer. In this case, though, the homeowner said that she and her husband had walked the neighborhood before they built their home and spoke with current customers of the same builder. They were looking for information about the builder that could only come from current customers. The customers they spoke with in this particular neighborhood painted a rosy picture of both the neighborhood and the builder. After closing, though, the homeowner reported learning of many problems afflicting houses in this neighborhood. It was clear that she and her husband would never have purchased their home had they known of the builder's habit of having this serious defect. In this case, the problem involved a defect in the construction of the home that caused moisture problems and consequential mold growth inside the home. The question here is why would "soon to be neighbors" not make this woman aware of a serious defect in the homes in this neighborhood (and spare her the pain that they were experiencing) until after she moved into her house? A possible explanation could involve the following:

- There were over 300 lots in this community
- The community was about half built-out
- Most of the residents were frequent movers
- All of the lots in the community were controlled by one builder

Does it make sense now? Everybody in the community knew about the problem but nobody wanted to say anything disparaging about either the community or the builder for fear that it would hurt sales, decrease property values, and thereby make it harder for them to sell their homes when they move. The lesson here is to gather as much information about the builder from numerous sources, not just the ones that you may think are the most reliable. In this case, the builder was publicly held and had disclosed the seriousness of the mold problem in a press release available to anyone who wanted to know.

Read the Fine Print

It is hard to glean from sales material how the builder will actually treat you if you do decide to buy one of their homes. You should talk to current customers, of course, but the builder may show their true colors in their own words. Read the builder's warranty, purchase contract, and any policies they have in place. For example, the sales brochure may suggest that you are welcome to visit your home at anytime while it is under construction. But if the builder has a policy banning you from the construction site without being escorted by a builder representative, you know they are not as forthcoming as the sales material may suggest. If their purchase contract is eight pages long and has very fine print, they may be hiding something. If their warranty has more exclusions and limitations than a sweepstakes, it's quite likely you are in for some trouble down the road.

An important concern is the extent to which the home builder will allow you access to inspect the home as it is being built. In short, your salesperson should confirm (in writing) that you are welcome to visit the home anytime. Due to safety considerations, the builder may require you to wear a hard hat, or tell you that they prefer that you visit during working hours. This is normal and expected. If they tell you that you are only welcome (or need) to see the home during a few, prescheduled times, *you should be very leery!* If the builder seems like they are trying to hide something… they probably are!

How Financially Stable Is the Builder? ♦WWW♦

Always look into the financial stability of your builder. If they are a publicly held company, the information is easy to get. Just look under "Investor Relations" on their Web site and you will be able to get their ticker symbol. You can take this symbol to an independent site like www.forbes.com and gather financial information. Publicly traded homebuilding companies are, as are all public companies, required to disclose financial information. Study the financial disclosures in either their Form 10-Q (quarterly Securities and Exchange Commission filing) or Form 10-K (annual report). It is amazing that some customers ignore clear warning statements explaining a company's financial problems. To illustrate this point, here is an excerpt from one home builder's Form 10-Q:

> *In the event the banks do not agree to provide waivers or otherwise amend the credit agreements and accelerate payments due per the agreements, the Company will encounter great difficulty in meeting the demands of the banks and will need to evaluate various forms of financial reorganization, the most severe of which could include bankruptcy.*

This particular company was nearly bankrupt and people were still buying their homes! And don't think this was because of a recession or weak housing market. This builder was operating in some of the hottest markets in the country at the peak of the housing boom. And don't be fooled by a builder touting their company's longevity. The builder mentioned above touted the fact that they were one of the largest regional builders, traded on the NASDAQ, and in business for over thirty-five years. In the course of a year they were "delisted" from NASDAQ, nearly bankrupt, and ended up selling what was left of the company to a competitor. Don't be fooled into thinking this can't happen to your builder.

Don't be mistaken by the size of a home builder when judging their financial stability. Surprisingly, builders work on thin profit margins (relative to the cash outlay), so poor management can lead to instability, regardless of size. Even if the builder is large and financially stable, they may decide to leave a city. I saw one of the largest builders in the country enter a new market, leave once they ran into some problems with their houses, return several years later, and then leave again! This was all in the matter of three years! Another builder would simply leave several service technicians in a city once they closed operations. You can bet those were some motivated employees! In that case, at least the builder made an attempt to honor their warranty. But even then, only the bare minimum was done for the customers. In the worst cases, some builders just go belly-up and close their doors.

While shopping the competition in one of the nation's biggest housing markets, I was surprised to find a moving truck in front of the model home of one of the area's largest builders. It turned out the builder was going out of business, leaving a half dozen homes (just in that community) unfinished. The locals may have known that it was coming, but being from out of town, I had no idea. What if you were relocating to that area? Would you have known that the builder was on the verge of bankruptcy?

I have seen some of the ugly realities of a struggling homebuilding business. You don't want to be one of their customers when the ship is sinking and a builder is under pressure to sell houses, meet their loan requirements, satisfy payroll, and finally to pay the subcontractors. It becomes no real secret on the job site when a company is in trouble. Subcontractors who are not being paid either refuse to work, or if they do show up, are very vocal about not being paid. When supervisors question why the "subs" aren't being paid, the company's position is: "It's either them or you." Surprisingly, most customers are oblivious to what is going on. Behind the scenes, the tensions are high. Customers are asked to move up the closing on their homes so that the company can get their money faster. The supervisors push to move jobs along quickly, using whatever labor they can find. The end result is a batch of homes that are quickly slapped together using a disgruntled group of subcontractors who are not committed to a top quality job. Most customers become aware of the situation only after they move in and realize the poor quality of the home they purchased.

The Web contains numerous stories about builders' financial problems. Check out our links page for one story about how homeowners were left without clear ownership of their new homes, even though some paid their builder for their homes in full -- with cash. **♦WWW♦**

In this day of mergers and acquisitions, don't presume that the building industry is immune. There may not be much you can do about it, but be aware that if your builder gets bought, policies and practices could change. This may not affect your home (unless you don't have what you were promised in writing) but it will likely affect the feel of the neighborhood if the new builder has a different product.

A homeowner in Nashville, Tennessee, signed a contract with a local "custom builder" that was later bought out by one of the largest production builder in the country. He was outraged to see the changes the new builder made to his neighborhood. You can find a link to his Web site on our links page.

Researching Smaller Builders ◆WWW◆

If you are dealing with a smaller builder where financial information is not readily available, you can still do a little detective work. You can find out from the applicable municipality if any liens have been filed against the builder or their subcontractors (public information in most jurisdictions). You can ask some of the subcontractors on the job or the builder's supply houses if the builder has a good reputation. If no one is willing to offer an opinion of that builder, beware. However, most people will be more than willing to share positive information such as which builders pay on time or who they believe builds a quality house. And don't forget the Better Business Bureau and the Attorney General's office in your state. If you are comparing several different builders, request reports on all of them. You may be surprised by what you find.

Consumer Protection Agencies

In the course of researching the material for this book, we reviewed complaints filed with the Better Business Bureau (BBB) and our state's Attorney General (AG) office for the largest builders in our state. I recommend that you request reports on the builders you are considering from either the BBB or the AG or both before you choose a builder. Watch out for red flags such as one builder with a large number of serious complaints filed against them relative to the number of homes built. In fact, we came across complaints against one builder that were so numerous the builder actually used a form letter to answer all of the complaints made to the BBB and AG!

We noticed two extremes in the types of complaints filed with the AG's office. One category consisted of serious, legitimate complaints involving the structural integrity or habitability of a home. Other complaints were trivial and contradicted the contracts agreed to by the homeowner and the builder. For example, customers would frequently complain about small defects that, as the homeowner described them, were within the tolerances set forth by the Industry Standards.

Industry Insight: *Industry Standards*

A new home is supposed to be built to "code" in order to meet the requirements of the municipality where the home is located. After you move into the house, though, the guidelines by which defects are judged change. Many builders use either an industry standards manual or something similar in their warranty to judge defects and tolerances. If the builder is using a standard created by another builder, you can guarantee that cases will crop up where you don't agree. For example, you may have a garage floor with a half dozen quarter-inch cracks in it after just six months. If those cracks are within the tolerances that your builder set forth and you agreed to at closing (maybe unknowingly) then you are out of luck. The industry standard or warranty may say that cracks in concrete are acceptable, as long as they are less than a half-inch in width. So before you sign on the dotted line, make sure you understand the standards by which defects that you will certainly encounter will be judged.

HomeBuilding
PITFALLS

Chapter Four:

Researching Your Neighborhood

As you read earlier, beyond researching the builder, it is also important to get a feel for the neighborhood. You want to make sure your kids have playmates -- or that the neighborhood has no kids if that is your preference. While this may be common sense, you may not be aware of the growing number of rules and regulations in new communities.

Subdivision Regulations
In most, if not all new communities, regulations govern everything from the type of structure that can be built on a piece

of property and the color you can paint that structure to the type and number of pets you are allowed and what happens if one of those pets has a litter! These regulations are often more restrictive and specific than the normal building codes and ordinances set forth by a city or county. Builders and developers have created these regulations to protect their investment until the community is finished or "built-out" and to protect the value of individual homes for their customers. Be sure you get a copy of the subdivision regulations from your builder or developer. Most importantly, <u>read and understand</u> them before you make any purchase decisions.

CCRs (Covenants, Conditions, and Restrictions)

The communities' rules and regulations created by the builder or developer take form in a document usually called the Declaration of Covenants, Conditions, and Restrictions. This is a lengthy public document filed with the county government or local municipality. Because there are national organizations and local real-estate attorneys that specialize in these documents, you should see commonalities in the language of CCRs. These documents are usually referenced in your purchase agreement, so make sure you and your attorney read and understand them. Unfortunately, you can't change anything in these documents without the support of the other property owners. Your attorney can't write in an addendum to your purchase agreement exempting you from the "offensive color" clause!

While you may not have grown up in a community with such strict regulations (for example, governing what color your house was or what pets you could or could not have) you may find some of the rules quite funny, intrusive, or controlling. Many of today's new homes are built in large, master planned communities with amenities such as play fields, pools, or golf courses. In such cases, rules need to be clearly established about how the community will be governed. Unfortunately, these documents can't just say:

> *We have a lot of stuff in this community; it needs to be taken care of, and nobody better paint their house purple.*

Instead, attorneys churn out sometimes hundreds of pages where they spell out the intent of the developer:

> WHEREAS, *the Declarant desires to provide for the preservation of the values and amenities in said community and for the maintenance of said common areas; and to this end, desires to subject the real property described in Exhibit "A" attached hereto to the covenants, conditions, restrictions, easements, charges, liens, hereinafter set forth, each and all of which is and are for the benefit of said Property and the subsequent Owners thereof...*
> -From the CCR of a community in Warren County, Ohio

The articles usually follow the same order. First, they define some of the common terms that will be used in the document such as "Living Unit," "By-Laws," or "Common Areas." Next the document spells out how the organization that governs the community (the Homeowner's Association or HOA) will be created and operated, to whom the rules apply and how much each member will be assessed initially and on an ongoing basis. Finally, the document spells out the actual rules and regulations of the community.

Here are some common articles found in declarations and common problems associated with each:

1. Definitions

The terms used in the declaration have meanings specific to the document. These terms may be new to you (such as "Common Area," "Private Access Roadway," or "Easement"). It may surprise you that the definition for "Common Area" describes not only the pretty recreational area, but also the ugly storm water retention area. Another example is where a "Private Access Roadway" is really a nice way of phrasing "shared liability and maintenance."

2. HOAs (Homeowners Associations)

If you have never lived in a newer community, an HOA (Homeowners Association) may be foreign to you. The HOA resembles a mini city council. It is usually set up as a nonprofit organization and has a president, vice president, and board members that chair different committees. The organization enforces the regulations set forth in the subdivision bylaws and regulations and also makes critical decisions about the maintenance of common property. The role of the HOA becomes much more important when a lot of common property exists such as pools, hiker-biker trails, play fields, tennis courts, and the like. Most newer, larger communities have many amenities that are the responsibility of the HOA to maintain. Usually in the beginning stages of the community, the developer or builder controls the HOA until enough homes are sold to allow for the hand-off of control to the homeowners. When the hand-off occurs (if not earlier) an election takes place for the president and board members of the HOA.

The funds needed to pay for the upkeep of common property are derived from fees collected from homeowners.

Depending on the amenities in the community, the fees will vary. But they will either be spelled out in the subdivision regulations or should be supplied in writing from the builder or developer. Make sure you know if the community has an initial contribution, annual assessment, individual, or special assessment. The HOA fees may be greater for specific lots if, for example, several lots share a common driveway that requires ongoing maintenance.

Although the bylaws may spell out caps on annual assessments, they may also allow special assessments at any time. Keep in mind that most HOAs have an increase in fees or special assessments over time. For example, if a problem occurs with the pool early on in a community, the developer will usually take care of it. What happens in a few years when the developer has severed ties with the community and the filtration system on the pool needs to be replaced? Without substantial reserves in the HOA's coffers, a special assessment must be made to cover the unplanned repair.

Finally, you should be made aware that HOA politics can damage neighborhood friendships. This may seem insignificant, but if your spouse wins a hotly contested post on the HOA over one of your neighbors, don't think the friendship will be unaffected. What if one of your neighbors is spending HOA money inappropriately? I know of a case where a homeowner was using common funds from the HOA to landscape (for his benefit) a common area directly behind his house. His neighbors all knew, but they didn't know how to approach him about it and still be able to remain "good neighbors." You should handle these situations much like you would in the workplace. Don't get caught up in the rumor mill, don't sweat the small stuff, but also don't let someone take advantage of his or her position of power.

3. Property Rights ♦WWW♦

The foremost reason why the CCR is written is to protect the developer of the property. He or she wants to make sure that the value of the property is retained throughout the course of the development period (from the sale of the first lot to the last). While the developer wants to protect the rights of future homeowners, special rights are also given to the developer and builder in the Declaration. Those rights include exempting themselves from some rules, but most importantly, controlling the HOA and having the right to change the bylaws as long as the developer and builder control most of the property, and usually beyond such a date. Most HOAs have two classes of members: the developer and the homeowner. The developer's votes usually count for at least the majority but can reach as much as 75 percent until such time as the developer owns less than a certain percentage of the lots. Sometimes the developer retains sole control of the HOA and the right to amend the declarations for as long as they own property within the community (in the form of lots to be sold to customers).

As a homeowner, you want to make sure that you understand all of the special property rights granted to the developer, builder, neighbors, and others with respect to your property. When I worked for a builder/developer, not one homeowner I dealt with clearly understood all of the rights, easements, liens, and encumbrances marked on the plot plan for their lot. Of course rules and regulations vary by community, but make sure you understand what easements apply to your lot and what those easements mean. You should have an attorney involved before you make a purchase decision, so make sure he or she explains such matters to you.

Special attention is merited if you live on a golf course, or any heavily "amenitized" community. You <u>must</u> clearly understand the rights of not just your neighbors, the builder, and the developer, but also the rights that the golf course owner, grounds crew, and the users of the facilities have over your property. For example, you should review the rules as to whether or not a golfer can come onto your lot to retrieve his golf ball that just hit your house (and damaged it, by the way). Of the CCRs I reviewed, the homeowner indemnifies the developer, HOA, course owner, players, swimmers, runners, maintenance workers, course architect, (let's just say everybody) for any loss or damage resulting from any of their activities not clearly negligent.

Picture a fairly typical community that includes a walking trail, a pool, and a public golf course. Imagine you are having party at your home that overlooks the ninth green. What happens if one of your guests goes onto the fairway to practice his chipping? What if this same guest has a horrible slice and one of his shots ricochets off of a tree, bounces off the walking trail, and strikes a child in the community's pool? Will the parents of the child sue you, the HOA, or your guest with the bad golf swing? Will the HOA sue you? Will you sue me? It's an extreme example to make a point, but either know your risks before you close on your house or speak with your insurance agent to ensure that your homeowner's coverage extends to include these additional risks imposed by the CCRs.

Before moving on, consider one more little item to confuse things and to make you even more cynical. You may be looking at a community that three months ago was a cornfield. You may have been listening to a salesperson describe what the community will look like in a few years. Picture the salesperson describing to you a "golf course community with walking trails and a community pool." He even hands you a full-color copy of the community plan describing all of the amenities and a thick booklet that explains how all of these common areas will be maintained. But when you get home, you read the booklet titled "Declaration of Covenants, Conditions and Restrictions and Reservation of Easements for _____ Subdivision" and you notice a little paragraph tucked away that reads:

> *Declarant* (in this case the builder/developer selling the lot and home) *does not warrant or represent that any recreational facilities will be constructed by or on behalf of Declarant. In determining whether to construct any recreational facilities, Declarant may consider whether the construction at the time of making the decision would be economically feasible in light of the then existing economic conditions, whether Declarant has sufficient funds available for the construction, whether the operation, maintenance and repair of the recreational facilities as constructed will be adequately funded by the assessments, including any increase to the assessment as provided in this Declaration. Declarant may also consider other factors.*

You see where I am going with this. The developer has made no promise and does not actually have to build what he says he is going to build. Can you do much about it? Probably not. I witnessed one community rise up around a piece of property that was promised to be a golf course. The developer went belly-up and left million-dollar homes overlooking narrow strips of weeds. Bottom line: Read the fine print.

4. Architectural Control

One of the ways a builder or developer controls the feel of a community and retains his investment is by way of architectural control. Architectural controls mean that the community has a set of guidelines explaining in general or in detail what types of structures can be built in a community. If you are buying a home from a production builder, chances are they either wrote the rules or are in compliance with them. You need to be most concerned with the rules only when you decide to change something on your home.

You may want to put in a pool after your house is built, or build a shed, deck, playhouse, fence, or even paint your house a different color. If this is prohibited, you need to know about it ahead of time. You may be thinking you understand you need approval to build a wall around your house, but you shouldn't have to go before a board if you want to paint your house a different color than the two choices the builder gave me. Wrong. You may very well have to go before the board, and the board that you go before is subjective. They may deny your request simply because your house is on a corner lot near the entrance to the community and it may "stand out" too much. Ahh, remember good old American freedom and individuality?

Although I joke about the socialist nature of HOAs and CCRs, they are rooted in good intentions. Most new home buyers today are frequent movers who want some predictability in their neighborhood. They want to know that when it is time to move again in a few years, their investment will be protected.

You should be aware of the consequences of not complying with the bylaws, especially for two reasons. First, you want to know the cost to you if you break the rules. Second, you want to be sure that the bylaws have some teeth for protecting the value of your home if one of your neighbors breaks the rules. If your neighbor breaks the covenants and restrictions by building an eight-foot-tall privacy fence and the bylaws are not enforced, they may as well not exist.

Keep in mind, the chance also exists that the builder or one of his successors can change the restrictions while they still retain majority ownership of the lots or votes. For example, if a builder is building high-end homes and they are not selling well, he may make the restrictions less stringent and begin building smaller, less expensive homes. By changing the restrictions in a community, the builder has sold more homes, but at a lower price, bringing down the overall value of all the homes in the community.

Amusing Restrictions

Seeing as the average new home price in this country is over $200,000, it amazes me that we still need restrictions that ban the raising of livestock. Do you think that without such a restriction, most suburbanites would be raising cattle in their backyards? Here are some interesting restrictions I have come across. You can laugh now, but wait until you read the restrictions for your community!

- No oil drilling, quarrying, or mining operation shall be permitted on any lot. (The lots in this community were all less than a half acre.)
- The maintenance, keeping, boarding, or raising of animals, livestock, or poultry of any kind, regardless of number, shall be and is hereby prohibited on any lot.
- Notwithstanding the above, in the event such household pets have a litter, the owner shall have a period of one hundred twenty (120) days from the date of such birth to dispose of such excess pets.

5. Easements

Easements are restrictions placed on your property, usually for access by municipalities (for streets, sidewalks, or drainage) or utility companies (for electricity, telephone, or cable lines). These areas of access or "right-of-way" are shown on your plot plan (see next section). For example, it would be unrealistic for a utility company to ask your permission every time they wanted to access equipment installed on the edge of your property. This same logic applies to your sidewalk. Although it is on your property, other residents in your community can use it without your permission.

You need to pay special attention to easements affecting your property and be sure that your attorney explains the meaning of each one. You do not, for example, want to build a play structure for your children in a drainage easement in your backyard. If the developer has to drive a bulldozer through your backyard to establish a swale to ensure proper drainage for your neighbor's lot, the easement you accepted by purchasing the home and lot may have given the "'dozer operator" permission to turn your elaborate swing set into toothpicks.

Understanding Shared Utilities

For the most part, municipalities maintain the utilities in a new community. If all you have to do is send in a check for your water and sewer, be thankful.

If a private wastewater treatment plant will handle your wastewater, be sure to get the details of the agreement and have them reviewed by a real estate attorney before you sign a purchase agreement. Private systems are fine until something goes wrong and repairs need to be made or they need to be expanded. Just like any shared resource in the community (pools, parks, running trails) you need to be aware of where the maintenance responsibility lies. Remember, if a pump needs to be replaced in a large municipality's water system, the cost can be spread over thousands of customers. If a pump breaks in your small 150-lot community, you may be in for a surprise!

If your home is on a well and/or septic system and municipal water/sewer is planned in your area, you may be **required** to hook up to the service. That seems fine, if the municipality is footing the bill, but in most cases, the cost associated with tying into the system is the responsibility of the property owner! That can be thousands of dollars! More than likely, any cost associated with the hook-up will be offset by the increase in property value, but you need to be prepared for the initial expense.

HomeBuilding
PITFALLS

Chapter Five:

The Model Home

You have heard it a thousand times: your home will probably be the single largest investment you ever make. It stands to reason that your new home purchase will involve one of the biggest sales pitches you ever get. Understanding the sales process before you step into the model home will put the ball in your court and help you keep control of the process. Good salespeople are savvy enough to judge your experience and knowledge related to buying a new home and look for weaknesses to exploit. Contrary to their pitch, they are not there to be your friend or advocate.

It is never a good idea to completely trust what a salesperson is telling you or what you read in sales literature. You are better off to ignore most claims of product superiority, because many salespeople will be less than forthright. In one city, I talked to salespeople from two different home builders who claimed that J.D. Power and Associates rated their company number one in customer satisfaction. No, there wasn't a tie. One of them wasn't telling the truth.

There are steps in the sales process that a good salesperson will follow. Larger builders put their salespeople through formal training courses designed by new home selling professionals. If these salespeople are experienced, they will try to take you on a path that starts when you enter the model home and ends when you close the deal. They want to be in <u>control</u> of the entire process by giving you the information that will lead you to purchasing a home from them.

Understanding Sales Lingo
Salespeople like to use terms that will help them sell their product to you. They try to use phrases that will increase your <u>emotional involvement</u> with their product, and there is not necessarily anything wrong with this. Salespeople everywhere use similar tactics. I raise this issue so that you are aware of it and can <u>maintain an objective view</u> as you evaluate what these people tell you. Here are some examples:

- They will always call their product "your new home" instead of a "house"
- They will say "community" instead of "neighborhood"
- They will say "your new home site" instead of "lot"

Before You Even Walk Through the Door: Pitfalls of the Emotional Hook.

One of the main advantages that a production builder has over a smaller custom builder is their ability to market on a larger scale. The most tangible example of this is the model home. Without a model home, a customer is forced to imagine how a home will be laid out and how it will fit with their lifestyle. But when that customer can walk through a home similar to the one that could be built for them, the first hook is set in place -- emotional involvement.

I have been in dozens of model homes across the country and have found myself a bit excited almost every time I opened the door. The soaring entryways, beautiful color schemes, impeccable decorations are all designed to grab your attention early on in the sales process so that you ultimately say, "We'll take it!"

There is nothing wrong with getting emotionally involved very early on in the sales process -- that's expected. You should feel like your new home will really fit you well. Just know that when it comes time to make the deal, you will be better off if you can separate yourself from the purchase. As you will see, the salesperson has <u>control</u> when they are <u>selling on emotion</u>.

Industry Insight: *Take a step back.*

In my experience dealing with serious warranty issues and product defects for a large builder, I visited hundreds of recently built homes. I learned how people use their homes, how they decorated, but most interestingly, who could actually afford their homes. These were considered luxury homes and had luxury prices...and some people were in over their heads. Some would be living in their homes for over a year and still be without furniture for most of the rooms. If you can't afford the

---

furniture and you don't even use the room, did you need the room? There was also another issue: when something went wrong, those who were financially in over their head were least equipped to deal with a crisis.

Some homeowners were very honest with me. They would admit that "this stupid house" was causing more problems in their life than they could have anticipated. Besides the fact that their home had problems, they bought a house they couldn't afford (or as some said, they were sold more house than they needed). They wanted to just sell it and move on, but they had to have their house fixed first. Unfortunately for one group of homeowners I was working with, their problem took over a year and a half to correct. Bottom line: Don't talk yourself into more house than you need. It will only cause problems for you in the future.

The hook!

Larger builders know how to set that hook using the model home as bait. Most model homes employ a steering technique that was perfected on farms to guide livestock into pens (that's how it feels anyway). If you have been to a few model homes, you know what I mean. Most builders convert the garage of the model home into a sales center and make you walk through that sales center to gain access to the home instead of going through the front door. It is in that sales center where you will most likely be introduced to the salesperson for the community or one of their assistants.

Model homes are decorated in a way that demonstrates the benefits of the floor plan but mask the home's imperfections. The model home will generally display every option available in the home, but in so doing confuses the potential buyer as to the real cost of the home. To confuse things further, some builders use high-end "designer options" unique to the model home that are not even offered by the builder on a standard production home. In most cases, home buyers do not "deck out" their home to the extent that home builders do in their model home. The price of a "loaded" model home is not only too high for many customers, but impractical. As a rule, it is never a good idea to have the most expensive home in the neighborhood, as the models tend to be. If the builder displayed the home with the options that most people really purchase, the home would seem common or boring and would not be as enticing to the customer.

Turn the Tables: Take Control!

If you have to walk through the sales trap to get to the model home, use it to your advantage. Ask the salesperson to supply you with the following:

- a floor plan
- specifications sheet (spec sheet)
- standard features sheet
- a list of features included in the model home you are about to tour

Here is a list of other documents you will eventually need to get from the builder (these documents are explained in more detail later):

- purchase contract, along with Standard (preprinted) Contingencies and Addendums
- copy of the warranty
- standard closing forms and any other legal documents you will ever have to sign
- copy of the neighborhood Covenants, Conditions and Restrictions
- copy of the Homeowner's Association Manual
- plot plan

Try to collect as much information about the builder as you can at this point. It will help you with some of the exercises mentioned later in the book.

Use the included features sheet to ensure that items are included and to create a baseline when performing comparative analysis with similar homes ("comps"). For instance, one builder may include a concrete back patio and another might not even mention the patio because it is not included in the price. This way you can compare apples to apples when looking at price.

Ask the salesperson to tell you the major differences between the model home and the standard plan. The salesperson who hesitates in answering this question is trying to hide the fact that the model has many upgrades. Find out before you step through the door if the model includes:

- optional living space such as a "bonus room," finished lower level, a "sun room," or additional bedrooms
- higher ceilings or other expensive structural features
- additional windows and doors
- "bump outs" to the original floor plan.

"Bump outs" are additions to a room that add square footage to the home. An additional bay window in the kitchen or additional floor space added to a living room that extends out behind the house are common options. Be aware that the cost per square foot of these "bump outs" will probably be higher than the rest of the house.

Most people know when they go through a model home that the furniture, the whole-house audio system, and even the fake fruit are not included in the price of the home. However, if you walk into the kitchen and see an eating area, you would expect that to be included in the price. But you may be wrong. Have that information before you walk into the model home, and don't forget to consider the outside of the model home. If the builder offers optional elevations (exterior designs), they may be on display with the model home. The home might be upgraded with brick, stone, or stucco when the standard is only vinyl. Your assumption that even simple things (like gutters) are included may be wrong. Do the research and know what you are actually buying.

The trap many people fall into is that they fall in love with the model that "starts in the low $200's" but is shown with all the upgrades and goodies that would cost $300,000 to duplicate (even without the fake fruit). As the price begins to inch upwards, people get emotional and begin justifying or selling themselves on their ability to afford that home. This is a bad move.

Flaws masked
A number of tricks used in decorating a model hide some problems with the design of the home or highlight some impractical option. The most common tricks happen in the bedrooms to make them seem larger or more functional.

Decorators will:

- use smaller scale furniture
- leave out pieces of furniture like dressers or desks
- make a bedroom into an office or sitting area, masking the fact that you could never comfortably fit a bed and other furniture in the room!
- use a whimsical theme such as a jungle look, thus allowing the decorator to, for instance, exchange a hammock for a bed

Some builders remove the interior doors in the model to make the rooms flow together and give the illusion of larger space. This also masks design flaws, such as a situation in which one door has to be closed before another door can be opened.

Before you fall in love with the beauty of an option, take a step back and look at its practicality. For example, builders sometimes place a soaker or whirlpool tub against a bank of large, expensive windows. This looks very appealing in a model, and therefore may help to set the emotional hook, but it's not always practical. Unless you don't mind entertaining your neighbors, you wouldn't be able to enjoy the windows because you would have to cover them if you ever planned on using the tub (especially in a first-floor master bedroom).

Many people do not notice any imperfections in a model home because the fancy painting, wallpaper, and decorating captivate attention and mask flaws. The next time you are in a model home, take a closer look at the details. Look behind doors for imperfections in paint or for cracks in the drywall. Take a close look at the hardwood floors for poor cuts, cracks, or scratches. Take a look at the bath area for cracks in the tile grout or scratches in the bathtub. Builders generally spend extra time trying to correct these imperfections. If you look closely, you will find them. Some customers don't look for these imperfections in the model, but are then outraged when they find them in their new home. Don't be naïve. Models have cosmetic flaws, and your new home will, too.

To get the best representation of a builder's finished product tour a house that is nearly complete. You will be much better served to tour a market or "spec" home of the floor plan that has captured your interest. This will give you a better idea of the actual quality of the finished product.

HomeBuilding
PITFALLS

Chapter Six:

Pitfalls of the Sales Process

Besides the tangible sales tools, such as the community itself and the model homes, the one-on-one sales process begins when you meet the salesperson (community representative, sales associate, Vice President of Sales, or whatever their title may be). They have to first sell *themselves* and then the:

- company
- geographic area
- community
- model or floor plan
- lot or home site

You will likely hear a similar spiel from each salesperson:

- Our company is committed to quality and customer satisfaction
- The area is great, close to schools and shopping
- The community offers wonderful amenities
- We have a home that will fit your lifestyle

Qualifying

Your salesperson will try to convince you that you need to buy a home from him or her. The information you get from the salesperson will be based on your responses to questions they ask you when they "qualify" you. You will know you are being qualified when you are asked questions like:

- How long have you been looking for a new home?
- Where have you been looking?
- What is keeping you from making up your mind?

These opening questions will either lead to a brush-off (at which time the salesperson wishes you good luck in your house hunting) or will set up more probing questions. Obviously, if you are just in the model looking for design ideas and have no interest in the area or the home, you will get the brush-off. If, however, you tell the salesperson that you are looking for a home in that area at the price range that is offered in that neighborhood, the salesperson will further qualify you.

In-Depth Qualifying

Once the salesperson feels that you are generally interested in what they have to offer, they will ask questions so they can build a path that will end with you buying a home from them. Each question will have a purpose:

Where do you currently live?
　　To classify you: relocator, local move-up, second home

What have you seen that you liked or disliked since you started looking?
　　This tells the salesperson what they are competing with and also allows them to focus on the aspects of their products that best fit what you are looking for (which might be completely different than what they told their last customer)

How soon had you planned on moving into your new home?
　　Reveals the urgency of your decision. The salesperson can then decide if they need to create a "fear of loss" (explained later)

What do you do for a living?
　　Lead-in to financial ability questions

Have you investigated financing options?
　　Are you candidates for their own mortgage company?

How much do you plan on putting towards a down payment?
　　What can you afford?

Once the salesperson knows that you are both interested in buying a new home in that area, and more importantly, can afford the price range that they are selling, the game is on! The salesperson will now try to find the right combination of floor plan and home site to meet your needs. The questioning will now shift from finances to lifestyle.

- What type of home are you looking for: formal, informal, open?
- Are you married?
- How large is your family, or how large are you expecting it to be?
- What do you like and dislike about your current home?
- What would you change about your current home?
- Which of our model homes do you like the most?
- What was it about Builder X's model that you liked?

It is at this point when you'll notice the difference in salespeople. You can begin to judge how well the salesperson knows their products and is attempting to serve your needs. Did the salesperson actually listen to your responses to all of the qualifying questions? A great salesperson will take everything you have said to this point, paying special attention to your "hot buttons" (need for a large family room, four bedrooms, etc.) and offer several home plans that meet your needs. A poor salesperson will lay out the dozens of plans offered in that community and have you choose which one you like. If the salesperson has a plan that seems to meet your needs on paper, you can then go visit it as a model or a home under construction to test the layout for yourself.

Choosing a Floor Plan or Model

Before you settle on a floor plan, make sure you have a clear understanding of the price of that model as you want it. This was mentioned earlier in the "Model Home" section of the book, but it deserves repeating: You must have an "Included Features" sheet from several builders in order to compare which features builders include in the standard home.

Industry Insight: *New Floor Plans*

If you chose a plan that is new and has not been built many times by the builder, you will be the guinea pig for finding out what the design problems are. Ask the builder how old the plan is and how many times it has been built. Try to avoid being a guinea pig by avoiding floor plans that are less than six months old.

If you are moving from one area of the country to another, be especially sure to understand what the builder considers "options." You may be moving from a warm climate where air-conditioning is standard. Understand that it is not standard everywhere. Don't think that just because you are in the market for a "luxury" home that everything is included. Have the builder supply a "standard features" sheet. Collect these from a number of different builders at different price levels to compare which features each builder considers standard. From the different lists you can compile a master list to bring to your builder. Before you sign a contract, confirm what is included in the purchase price.

This is an exercise that good salespeople and good builders go through in order to compare themselves to the other builders in the marketplace. I have performed hundreds of these "comps" between builders.

You need to do comps to know the strengths and weaknesses of each builder's model, especially if you are comparing two similar models from two different builders. This is good to do because you don't want to miss something that may be of high dollar value, such as one builder not including a full basement.

Selling the Home Site

Before you decide on that "perfect" lot, do your homework. Your builder should be able to supply you with a plot plan that shows the dimensions of the lot. If the municipality has approved the plot plan, it is a legal description of the lot dimensions. Don't simply rely on the marketing material supplied by the builder or developer to judge the quality or size of the lot.

On a plot plan, be sure to understand, or find someone who can help you understand:

- setbacks
- utility easements
- trees
- fill areas
- sewer elevation
- slope and drainage

Adjoining Property

If the lot you are considering is in the middle of the community and is surrounded by other homes, you have the typical boundary issues to worry about. But, if your lot adjoins common space (including green spaces, bodies of water, or drainage areas) watch out! Most of the complaints I have heard from homeowners about their lots are from those that didn't know what their lots were adjoining. Again, do your homework and don't rely on what a builder or the salesperson tells you. You want to know:

- Is that adjoining green space really just a lush field or is it designed to hold water runoff during storms?

- Is there really a daycare center planned for that commercial lot in my backyard or does the zoning allow for something else?
- Who is responsible for that nice planting area the developer built on the corner of my property?

If you don't find out before you build, it will be too late.

You don't want to find out after the fact that:

- That lush green space becomes an ocean when it rains and makes your yard unusable for weeks until it dries up.
- That commercial lot behind you was sold to a chemical distributor that built an ugly warehouse on the property. The noise from the trucks starts at 6 a.m. and lasts all day.
- When a drunk driver drove through the nice planting bed on the corner of your lot and damaged the decorative wall that the developer built, you found out that it was your responsibility to repair it. You knew that the area was a part of your property, but you didn't know that you were responsible for the damage.

These are just a few examples, but they are real. ♦ **WWW** ♦

You need to know the price of the lot the home will be built on in order to calculate the total price of the home. There are many factors that will influence the price of a home site. Your home may be built on a lot that was:

- developed by and is owned by the builder
- purchased by the builder from a developer
- will be purchased by the builder upon receipt of your deposit

This is where "lot premiums" come into play. Because no two lots in a community are the same, the builder can charge a subjective premium for lots that are perceived to be better. Now, of course, a larger or wooded or golf course view lot will garner more money than a plain flat lot. What if the entire community if full of plain flat lots? That is where the lot ratings become subjective.

If all things are held equal, you can make some generalizations about the value of different lots. Cul-de-sac lots are more desirable unless the lot is immediately at the end of a cul-de-sac and is subject to the headlights of vehicles coming down the street. Interior lots are perceived to be more "safe" because they are buffered from any property adjoining the community, especially if the adjoining property is undeveloped. The thinking is that you want to know what will adjoin your property. If it will simply be another house like yours, no problem, but if it's a wastewater treatment plant, bid property value goodbye.

Sometimes builders use monikers like "AAAA" or "Premium IV" to describe the values of different lots. You may never know the actual price of the lot, only the difference in the price of one lot over another. Because these values are subjective, room exists to bargain with the builder. Usually the cost of developing a lot is the same amount or is simply an average. Any premium placed on a lot is "gravy" for the builder.

There are several major milestones in the sales process. You may have already sold yourself on the geographic area. If the salesperson has sold you on the community and you have decided on a floor plan that you like, all they have to do is get you to fall in love with a lot.

> **Industry Insight:** *Have I got the lot for you!*
> If the salesperson has a large inventory of lots at his
> disposal, you may only be offered a few choices. The
> salesperson might be trying to avoid the possibility of
> "cherry picking" where the first buyers take all of the
> good lots and leave only the "tough sells." Allow the
> salesperson to show you lots that he thinks will meet your
> needs, but be sure to explore on your own to make sure
> that you make the right choice. The salesperson may tell
> you that they have just the right site for the home plan
> you have selected. What they actually have is several
> lots in mind. They are showing you the least desirable lot
> first. If you choose that lot, the salesperson has
> accomplished two goals. First, they have rid themselves
> of a less desirable lot. Second, they have left themselves
> with a lot offering more benefit to another prospect. And
> if you didn't like the first lot the salesperson showed you,
> he has others in mind that were more desirable anyway!

You may limit your choice of lots by choosing a home that will
only fit on a limited number of lots. If you choose a wide home
with a side entry garage in a community with a large number of
narrow lots, your choices are limited.

Remember, even in a neighborhood where the lots seem "cookie-
cutter," no two home sites are the same.

Overcoming objections: When you say this, they say that.
Before any deal can be closed, the salesperson must overcome
any objections that you have. During the sales process <u>you will
make compromises</u>. Maybe the family room in the home you
have selected is not as large as the competitors but the
community is nicer. Maybe the lots are not as large as the
"other" community you were looking at but they are a better

value. These are example of objections that the salesperson is trained to overcome.

In order to overcome objections that you will raise during the sales process, the salesperson will try to put a "spin" on the situation. They will try to convince you that the issues you raise are not insurmountable. Even the most inexperienced salesperson will be prepared for the common objections such as:

- your discomfort with a design element in the home.
- your displeasure with the price, which is more than you originally wanted to spend.
- your disappointment in the schools, which are not "top-tier" as you had hoped.
- your increased commute time because the community is farther from your workplace.

If you don't set your limits, you will make mistakes that could be costly. Go into the sales process knowing your limits for financial, personal, and family choices and be sure of what you are comfortable in settling on; don't let the salesperson do it for you! Don't let the salesperson convince you that:

- The home will "grow on you."
- Although it's more than you wanted to spend, the monthly payment will only be slightly more.
- Another ten minutes added to your commute time is no big deal.
- Although the schools are not "top-notch" you can send your kids to private schools.

The salesperson can address these issues individually, but they would rather just create a sense of urgency to motivate you to buy, even if you are not ready. The sense of urgency is triggered when the salesperson hears you say things like:

- We want to think it over.
- We want to sleep on it.
- We want to look at some other builders before we decide.
- It's more than we had planned on spending.

The salesperson wants you to believe that if you "sleep on it" you will miss out on an opportunity to own a unique property. They will tell you that prices will be going up soon, or that the lot you want is very popular and will probably be sold to someone else if you don't buy it soon. They are trying to create a "fear of loss."

It is also very common for salespeople to quickly attempt to persuade you to write a check to reserve that lot (most likely in the amount of $500 or more). They probably will not even cash the check. They simply want you to get the feeling that you have become financially involved in the purchase. They then have you both emotionally *and* financially involved. They know that most customers are less likely to back out of the sale once they have become that involved. It is better to step back and think it over (as well as continue to comparison shop) than succumb to a sales tactic and risk settling for less than you could have gotten elsewhere or committing to more than you can comfortably afford. Although it is always possible that a lot you like may get sold to someone else, nine times out of ten it will still be there in a week.

Again, a good salesperson will listen for your critical needs. If you are price sensitive, the fear of loss will be related to a price increase. If you need to have a home within a certain time frame, the fear of loss message will stress the urgency of beginning construction soon. If you "fall in love" with a certain lot, the salesperson will sense this and urge you to put down a deposit to reserve "your" lot.

> ## Industry Insight: *Regret and unrealistic expectations in overspending.*
>
> I mentioned earlier some of the problems that accompany spending beyond your means for a new home. One of those issues relates to the way problems seem to be magnified with a home that you can't afford. Another problem common with overspending is having unrealistic expectations for your new home. I remember talking to one angry homeowner about some of the defects in her new home. She told me that she and her husband paid $100,000 more than they had anticipated paying for a new home in hopes of avoiding the exact problems they were experiencing.
>
> The adage "you get what you pay for" is not always true in the homebuilding industry. You need to research the builder's reputation, no matter what you are paying for the home. Don't think you can expect perfection if you are paying top dollar for a new home. With large builders, there are frequently problems no matter how much you pay.

The Real Estate Agent

You may have been thinking: so what role does a real estate agent play in all this? To get a good understanding of what role a real estate agent plays, you need to follow the money trail. In a traditional agreement, the seller pays the real estate agent. When you buy from a builder, the builder pays your agent. This is a fair arrangement considering the agent put the buyer and seller together. You just want to make sure your agent is steering you to a builder for the right reasons.

Most savvy builders wine and dine the real estate community because without the support of agents, most builders would be out of business. Before the model homes open agents are feted with free brunches that come with plenty of giveaways. But that's just a few free meals, right? How about contests involving cell phones, fur coats, money, cars, and vacations? Did your agent bring you to the model home of a builder because they believe the builder will sell you a well-built house or was the agent only one sale away from winning a two-year lease on a Lexus?

Many people don't understand how aggressively builders court agents. The people that are most at risk of being misled are relocators. "Relo's," as they are called, are often naïve to the new home marketplace. You may be comfortable looking for a home on your own in a place you have lived all your life. On the other hand, you may rely on a real estate agent if you just transferred to a new city. Be sure to do your own research and talk to as many people you can (co-workers for example) and keep your options open before you narrow your search to a single builder.

www.HOMEBUILDINGPITFALLS.com

HomeBuilding
PITFALLS

Chapter Seven:

Options and Selections

After you have picked a floor plan and a lot that you like, you will need to go over the options that are available for that floor plan. You will need to do this before you can really get an idea of how much your new home will cost. <u>Never</u> sign a purchase agreement before you have performed your selections. Why would you agree to purchase something if you don't know what the price is?

Most builders offer a myriad of options and combinations:

- front vs. side entry garage
- tile vs. vinyl flooring
- extra rooms
- bump outs
- elevations or exterior designs of the house
- window packages, etc.

Most of these items are priced out on a per-item basis. Some, like an elevation or structural option, are all inclusive. For example, the price for a different elevation may include the cost of additional windows, cladding, changes to the foundation, etc.

Remember to avoid using the model home as an example of how your home will look. Most purchase agreements explicitly state that the model home is for display purposes only and is in no way a representation of the home that will be built for you. Even if your salesperson is honest, it is not uncommon for options to be left out of your home plans due to human error. You will have recourse against the builder only if you have everything in writing.

Industry Insight: *Comparing Apples to Apples*
As mentioned in Chapter Five, models are nice to look at, but a better example of the final product is a home of the same floor plan that is nearly complete. Try to tour one of the builder's homes that is nearly complete to get a better idea of what is included in the price. Have the salesperson give you a list of included features in the home and the contract price so that you can get a better understanding of what to expect.

Intelligent Selections

There are certain options that you should really consider at the time of selections. These features vary from area to area across the country, but all have one thing in common: they are much easier to install during the original construction phase. Remember, you can always add the decorative features later. You only get one chance to make structural decisions like:

- 9' vs. 8' ceilings
- three-car vs. two-car garage
- additional full bath vs. half bath
- larger electric service (200 amp vs.150 amp)

If you are working with a real estate agent, be sure to ask what features should be included in the home to make it more attractive on the resale market. Remember to weigh option selections and all decisions about your home based on the expected length of occupancy. The longer you plan on staying in the home, the less you have to cater to the resale market. If you are a frequent mover or transferee, you can't put too much of your personal stamp on the home.

The selection process usually takes place in either a model home, or in the case of larger builders, in a design or selection center. The design centers mimic retail stores in the sense that they display for comparison all the products that can go into your home (flooring, cabinets, fixtures, siding, etc.). You should know and understand that the "selections center" is in reality a profit center for the builder. The person taking you through the selections process is <u>making a commission from every upgrade</u> that you make. There is nothing wrong with this, but you need to be aware of it.

Many builders will try to get you to upgrade all the products you have chosen, which may seem like a pretty good idea to you after you see how cheap the standard selections are. Take carpet as an example. The standard carpet your builder offers you is usually a "contractor's grade" carpet with very thin fiber (about 25 oz.).

I have seen the reaction of more than one homeowner who experienced walking on their new carpet with bare feet (or with only socks on) for the first time. As they walked near the edge of a room, or placed their toes near the back of a stair while walking up the staircase, they were pricked by the "tack strip" (the strip of tacks that holds that carpet in place). They were amazed how thin the carpet was. They could not tell from looking at the small sample in selections that the carpet would feel so thin. ◆**WWW**◆

There are options that you should stay away from in selections. I recommend avoiding any option that is easily available (usually cheaper) from another company after the sale. Try to avoid options such as:

- garage door openers
- window treatments
- security systems
- water purifiers/softeners

You can almost always find these items much cheaper at a home improvement store or from another company after you move in. You will be told during the selections process "you can purchase those items here and not have to worry about them after you move in."

Another common sales pitch is that you can just "roll all these items into your 30- year mortgage." I'm not sure that paying for window blinds for thirty years is a very good idea!

HomeBuilding
PITFALLS

Chapter Eight:

Closing the Sale

You will know when the salesperson is trying to close the sale when they begin reviewing the stages you have been through and confirming your interest. The salesperson will use "tie-down" phrases to help you reassure yourself that you are making the right decision. A good salesperson will bring up things you have already sold yourself on:

- Can't you see yourself enjoying the community pool on a warm summer day?

- You will have a much more peaceful home when the kids have their own rooms, right?
- Isn't that a great lot for that home?

You may still be apprehensive at this point. If you only have a few minor objections, the salesperson will do or say whatever it takes to get you to sign the purchase agreement or put down a deposit.

Before you go any further, you will want to have several things from the builder (in addition to the "Included Features" sheet mentioned earlier). You will want to obtain copies of:

- the purchase contract (agreement), warranty, standard closing forms and any other legal documents (anything and everything you will be signing before, during, or after construction) for your attorney to review.
- the neighborhood Covenants, Conditions and Restrictions. As explained earlier in Chapter Four, CCRs spell out what can and cannot be built in your neighborhood.
- the Homeowners Association Manual outlining property restrictions and guidelines as well as any fees for neighborhood maintenance and improvements.
- specification sheet listing all materials that will be used in the house. This list should also include brand names as much as possible. Builders always leave the option for themselves to substitute materials with other "materials of equal or greater value" in the event that a certain brand name is not available at the time it is needed for your home.
- any standard forms and addendums the builder uses for inspections, radon testing, installation of your own security system, etc.

Industry Insight: *Stop Right Here*
Let me stop right here and reiterate a very important point. Do not even think of signing anything that relates to the purchase of a home without having your attorney review it first. Builders use preprinted forms that make their one-sided legalese appear fair. And don't even think of picking up that pen and initialing anything without reading Chapter Ten: Pitfalls of the Legal Process.

Next, you will want to finalize pricing. *Prices are almost always negotiable* (the exception to this may be in a hot market where homes are selling easily and fast). The way the salesperson presents the price of the home makes it seem like the price is set in stone. Don't ever be reluctant to make a counter offer. Remember, if you have made several high-dollar upgrades or are choosing a "premium" lot, you are in a good position to ask for five to ten percent off the asking price. The salesperson's first reaction will probably be to tell you that they cannot do it. Hold firm for a while. Money talks. If you tell them you will sign the agreement the minute they give into your price request, they will probably give in eventually (assuming your attorney is comfortable with the language in the contract). If they don't, you can always agree to the original price later.

Here is another negotiating tip. Waiting until the last minute to bring up the price discount will improve your odds of getting it. The salesperson is less likely to turn you down after they have already invested a great deal of time and effort into you during the selling process, because they have become involved with you at that point (the "getting too involved trap" works both ways)!

If you find the builder reluctant to move on the price, there may be several good reasons. In most cases, the selling price of a home is public information that is used by, among others, appraisers, to find comparable values. Just as you did a "comp" to find the best value when you were shopping for a home, a bank employs an appraiser to perform a similar exercise to determine a property's value. An appraiser doing a "comp" in a production home neighborhood has an easy job. He can simply find the most recent sale of a similar model to get a good comparison for the home he is appraising. What the builder does not want to do is allow a "Monticello" model to sell for less than a similar "Monticello" did in the past. What could happen is the comparables could drop and the next "Monticello" may not appraise for the buyer. If the bank doesn't approve the loan for the customer, a sale is lost and the builder is hurt.

If the builder is forced to make a price concession, they would prefer to do so by giving away options such as upgraded flooring, cabinets, or a finished upper or lower level (builder speak for finished basement or attic). There are other creative ways to lower the cost of the home purchase that benefit both you and the builder without hurting future price increases in the neighborhood. Remember, you want to see the builder do well after you close on your house so that your home will garner the most money on the resale market.

Keep in mind, your ability to negotiate on price, options, loan fees, etc., requires that you have leverage. If you intend on having a large number of contingencies, the biggest one probably being the sale of your present home, then don't expect the builder to budge too much. The negotiating game can be tough. You need to have a feel for the market conditions. You want to:

- build contingencies into the contract to protect yourself, but not so many that you don't have a strong negotiating stance.

- get the best price, but not so much lower that similar houses in the neighborhood appear overvalued.
- find a builder that will negotiate, but not one that is too desperate to sell a home because there is no sales momentum in the neighborhood. A poorly performing neighborhood will not retain its value and makes it harder for you to sell your home on the resale market.

Just as prices are never "written in stone," neither are down payments or deposits. You can often negotiate for a lower down payment. If they ask for ten percent, offer them five percent. Again, you will need to be firm on this. In the event that you are not happy with the cards the builder deals you, it is better to have fewer chips on the table to lose. A smaller down payment makes it less costly (at least financially but not always emotionally) to walk away from the deal if things go sour. A lower down payment will give you a strong bargaining position throughout the process.

www.**HOMEBUILDINGPITFALLS**.com

HomeBuilding
PITFALLS

Chapter Nine:

Shopping Observations

I have visited quite a few model homes over the years, primarily for the purpose of gaining market insight. As part of the research for this book, I toured the model homes of many of the country's largest home builders to gain a better knowledge of some of the techniques used by new home salespeople. I went through the selling process as far as I could without actually having to sign a purchase agreement or put down any deposit money.

In each sales encounter, I posed as a different type of buyer in order to elicit a different response from the salesperson. From builder to builder I would vary my interest in purchasing. When I told the salesperson I was "considering other builders" he or she would remember a "special promotion" that was coming up or say that they "must have misquoted the price." This scenario never happened when I appeared interested in only one builder.

I remember meeting a couple who had always aspired to own a home built by a certain homebuilding company that had a good reputation for building high-end homes. The couple only considered this one builder when it came time to build their dream home. Did they ever pay for it! Not only were they taken advantage of when it came to price, but they also learned that the builder's current quality of work didn't live up to the reputation of past performance.

As mentioned in Chapter Three, talk to as many people as possible who have bought a home from the builder you are considering. <u>Never buy a home without first talking to previous customers of the builder.</u> Try to randomly contact some people that live in the community you are considering. The salesperson of a good builder should be very comfortable with the idea of you randomly knocking on peoples' doors in order to ask them about their building experience. Contacting people who are on a salesperson's pre-made reference list may not give you an unbiased look into the reality of buying from that builder. Salespeople will naturally prefer that you to talk with their happiest customers. One salesperson gave me a phone list of what was supposed to be every customer in an entire community, and then told me to pick any of them. I was impressed, but I can't help but wonder if every customer made it onto that phone list, or if the list was put together without the phone numbers of unsatisfied customers.

If possible, try to talk to customers who have had their home built by the same construction supervisor that will be working on your home. I will talk about this in more detail later, but just remember that the construction supervisor is the person with the most direct influence on the quality of the end product.

Honesty and Integrity

As I mention several times, it is important to have all pertinent documents (specification sheet, purchase agreement, warranty, etc.) before you make a purchase decision. One salesperson would not give me a copy of their purchase agreement until I was ready to sign it (although he did say I could have a copy early enough that my attorney could look over it) and would not give me a copy of their warranty until closing! I wonder what they were trying to hide. Take that as a good indication of how the company does business. If they won't be straightforward with you during the sales process, just think of how unresponsive they will be if you sign the purchase agreement or actually build a home with them.

I must have been wearing my "I'm stupid" sign when I had my first meeting with one salesperson. He began to tell me about their 1-10 warranty. He said that they "offer a full one-year warranty, but unlike any other builder in the city, we stretch our warranty out for an additional nine years."

He tried to make it seem as if the same amount of coverage would extend for the full ten years. I will go into the details of the warranty in a later chapter, but to use an automobile analogy, he tried to pass off a "power-train" warranty as a "bumper-to-bumper" warranty.

Another technique used by salespeople is to make you think that something included standard on their home is an extra cost option on a competitor's home. One salesperson told me about a specific construction technique that his company uses to waterproof their houses. He made it sound like they were the only builder in the city using such a technique, while in reality, several other builders in the area were also practicing a very similar technique. Once I told him that I was considering one of these other builders, he quickly, yet reluctantly, admitted that the other builder used a similar construction technique. Here again, this salesperson probably assumed that I had limited construction knowledge and therefore would not realize that other builders were using his "special" technique. He then went on to "talk down" the builder I said I was considering. Here are some observations:

1. Many salespeople will say *anything* to get the sale. If you do not understand what they are saying, they could very well be lying.
2. If a salesperson tells you negative things about another builder, allow the other builder to give you his side of the story. The salesperson could very well be, you guessed it: lying.
3. If you have shopped several builders and have an understanding of the market, it will be harder for a salesperson to "blow one by you."

HomeBuilding
PITFALLS

Chapter Ten:

Pitfalls of the Legal Process

Large builders use lengthy contracts and addendums that usually contain language that contradicts statements and promises made to you by salespeople. Ironically, the contract you will have to sign specifically state: "verbal commitments made by any of the builder's representatives will not be honored by the builder." Make sure to read the entire contract and any addendums. If you have any questions, have your attorney review the document with you. Even if you think you understand everything in the contract, an attorney will be able to offer a different perspective on how the content of the document may leave you vulnerable.

The salesperson would like you to believe that the builder has gone through this process thousands of times using the same contracts and forms with all of their customers -- and they very well may have. But that doesn't matter. These documents are some of the most one-sided you will read, outside of your warranty (see Chapter Eleven). The contract heavily favors the builder.

Here are some egregious examples of text from typical "big builder" contracts:

> *Purchaser agrees to pay Seller upon <u>substantial</u> completion of the house.*
>
> *Escrow will not be allowed for <u>unfinished</u> interior work.*
>
> *Seller shall <u>attempt</u> to complete items on Pre-Settlement List (see Chapter Fifteen), but closing will not be delayed due to unfinished items, nor shall funds be escrowed.*

You pay the seller when the house is done. <u>Completely</u>. If the yard is not complete and it's the middle of winter, then you place money in escrow and release it upon completion of the yard in spring.

Here is an example of how the above excerpts from "big builder" contracts can come together in one house and create a huge problem for the home buyer:

A builder had a house just eighteen days from closing which still needed almost <u>all</u> exterior work: siding, concrete driveway, stoop, patio, and brick work including a full masonry fireplace. The eighteen days could have been sufficient time, considering the fact that the interior was nearly complete, but nobody could have predicted the eighteen days of record frigid weather that was about to descend on the area. Because the builder needed this closing before the end of the quarter (in order to meet their budget) they forced the supervisor and subcontractors to push on. Laying brick and pouring concrete in such cold temperatures compromised the quality of the job. The builder needed this sale and knew that the contract language would back him up if the buyer balked and refused to close on the house.

In the end, the house was complete enough to get a certificate of occupancy (the municipality had approved it for occupancy), but was in no condition to have a proper walk-through performed. But remember the contract excerpts from above?

> *Purchaser agrees to pay Seller upon* **substantial** *completion of the house.*
>
> *Escrow will not be allowed for* **unfinished** *interior work.*
>
> *Seller shall* **attempt** *to complete items on Pre-Settlement List, but closing will not be delayed due to unfinished items, nor shall funds be escrowed.*

The house was *substantially* complete, so the buyer had to pay the seller (builder). Money from the buyer could not be withheld to make sure the final items were complete because *escrow was not allowed.* But at least the builder would *attempt* to complete the home.

The above examples cover only one small section of most builders' purchase agreements. What about all of the other legal mumbo-jumbo favoring the builder which you will be agreeing to if you simply sign on their dotted line?

So you're thinking: "Well, these are glaringly obvious pitfalls, my spouse and I would never agree to these terms. I deal with attorneys every now and then at work. I bet I could just revise any language in the contract that I don't agree with."

OK. How about:

- Implied Warranties?
- Claims of Habitability, Workmanship, Fitness for a Particular Purpose, or Merchantability?
- Waiving demand for Specific Performance?
- Should you agree to Arbitration as your sole means of dispute resolution?

These are questions for a good attorney. These are not questions for your *very experienced* real estate agent or your buddy who just bought from the same builder. You need a competent attorney to protect yourself.

Finding a Good Real Estate Attorney

During the sales, selections, building, and closing processes, you will be required to sign a myriad of documents that were prepared by highly paid attorneys to protect the interest of the builder. Don't even think of signing any of these documents without having your attorney review them, no matter what your salesperson, real estate agent, family, or friends say.

But if you don't have a real estate attorney, how do you find one?

A good referral may come from another professional you have worked with in the past such as your accountant, legal counsel for the company you work for, or from your local Bar Association. Almost every Bar Association has a Lawyer Referral Service that can guide you to an attorney who will protect your rights when you are buying a new home. You can search the American Bar Association's site for the phone number or Web site of your local Bar Association. ♦**WWW**♦

Explain to the attorney referral service exactly what you need: a residential real estate attorney to review and revise contracts and addendums for the construction and purchase of a new home and to represent you at time of closing. They will be able to give you the names of attorneys who practice in this area and are willing to meet with you.

According to the Web site, the use of the lawyer referral service entitles you to a half-hour consultation with the referred attorney where you can decide if that person will be right for the job. In the initial consultation, you will want to make sure the attorney has a good deal of real estate experience, especially as it relates to residential property. Any experience the attorney has in new home contracts and building is a plus, but understand that most people do not use attorneys when they purchase a production home. They are not smart or prepared, but you are.

The cost for a competent attorney to review the documents you will have to sign throughout the homebuilding process is well worth it. It only makes sense to spend several hundred dollars to protect yourself in a several hundred-thousand-dollar transaction. If you think you can't afford an attorney to protect you, then maybe you should think twice about whether you can afford the house.

Contract Addendums

A solid purchase agreement or contract is the first line of defense to protect yourself throughout the homebuilding process, but there are other documents you will need to bring to the attention of your attorney. As mentioned before, you will want to gather as much of the builder's literature as possible early on in your visit to the model home or sales center. As you move further along in the process, you will need to have copies of the following documents for your attorney to review:

- purchase agreement
- warranty
- HOA (Home Owner's Association) and CCR (Covenants Conditions and Restriction) documents
- plot plan, with easements marked, of the lot you are considering
- standard preprinted Contingencies and Addendums

Your Ammunition against One-Sided Builder Contracts

Changes and additions made to the documents mentioned above are usually done so with addendums. Although I am not an attorney nor do I play one on TV, I am simply suggesting that these are things you should discuss with your attorney. There are several addendums that you will want to consider adding to you purchase agreement (all of these addendums will not necessarily apply to your situation):

1. **Addendum**: *The new home must appraise at or above the sales price.* With all of the tricky pricing I mentioned in Chapter Five, you will want to make sure that your home is perceived to be valued at or above the purchase price. The problem is that an appraisal can be subjective. Depending on whose side the appraiser is on, they can make the numbers "work" or make them come out in their favor. This is especially true if you are using the builder's lender. You want an independent appraisal to protect yourself. If you are building a unique, multimillion-dollar home and paying cash for it, an appraisal is unnecessary. There is no bank to worry about you overpaying and then getting stuck with a house they can't resell if they have to foreclose. More likely,

you will have a mortgage on your house, and a bank that cares what happens in the event of a foreclosure.

2. **Addendum**: *The new home site must pass all relevant tests* (perk test for a ground stability and/or septic system compatibility, radon test, soils test). You do not want to be stuck with a home on poor soil that causes your house to settle or your septic system to operate improperly.

3. **Addendum**: *The new home must be code compliant.* If you think this is a no-brainer, think again. Just because a municipal inspector signed off on your house does not mean that every aspect of the home's construction is compliant with building codes. This addendum is not a demand for something above and beyond what is promised by the builder or within industry standards. Rather, it is to ensure that you are getting what you pay for.

4. **Addendum**: *You have the right to review the actual plans prior to construction* (not just the sample version shown in marketing material). You can review the locations of switches, the swing of doors, height of ceilings, etc., but the real review will take place by your inspector. This is a good first step for your inspector, who will be making several site visits to become acquainted with the intended design of the house. Just as you will be preparing a packet of material for your attorney to review, your inspector will need similar help in performing his or her job. Your inspector will need a complete set of plans, specifications, and included features, your additional selections and changes, and plot plan.

5. **Addendum**: *Specifications and Materials List.* Make sure the spec sheet outlines color, model names, and model numbers, but also that it states that these <u>must be installed according to manufacturer instructions</u>. Your inspector will be able to see if the major installed components such as windows, doors, and shingles comply with manufacturers recommendations. I have seen plenty of windows and doors that leak because they were installed improperly, thus voiding the manufacturer's warranty. And wouldn't you know it, the builder's warranty either had expired or excluded coverage of that part of the home. Also demand that you be supplied with all warranties for installed components. If the components were installed correctly and the warranty is registered to you, you may be protected long after the builder's warranty expires. Most contracts state that materials may be substituted for those of greater or equal value, which is fine, but they may not be your choice of style. Simply add that <u>you must approve changes</u> in materials to avoid any problems.

6. **Addendum**: *The builder and customer will agree on the features of the lot that will be protected.* This is especially important if you chose a lot because of a particular feature, like a tree. If that tree is damaged, you should be compensated.

7. **Addendum**: *The home will be complete before closing.* If no loophole appears in the purchase agreement, one will surely surface on one of the last forms you sign: the "punch list" or whatever form is used to document items that need to be corrected before closing.

Binding Arbitration: Who Does It Help/Hurt?

One of the hot topics in real estate law today is the binding arbitration clause that big builders are using in their contracts. In a nutshell, binding arbitration keeps your problem with the builder out of a courtroom. In doing so, it saves time and money for both parties, but can end up limiting rights you would normally have if the case were argued before a judge and jury.

As I mentioned before, I am not an attorney and this is not intended to serve as legal advice, but rather my humble opinion. For specific questions, call your attorney.

> *Pros:*
> The biggest benefit to arbitration is that it allows for quick settlement of your dispute. Because it is quicker and (in the case of *binding* arbitration) final, there is less money spent on legal fees.

> *Cons:*
> If the arbitration you enter into with the builder is binding, the decision of the arbitrator is final; there are no appeals. If you don't like the ruling of the arbitrator, this is clearly a problem. Also, you will not have the benefit of twelve jurors that may be more sympathetic to your plight.

I had experience with a large builder that was sued regularly. The builder's legal strategy was to settle with no one. I saw cases go on for years without resolution. In the case of this builder, had the claims gone to arbitration, at least some chance of settlement would have been possible. In the end, the builder went bankrupt and a number of homeowners with serious claims never had any resolution to their problems. Instead, the homeowners were out thousands of dollars in legal fees and stuck with defective houses.

Industry Insight: *Legal Arm Twisting*

Most large builders have a great deal of legal expertise at their disposal and don't fear a lawsuit from a customer because the assumption is they have deeper pockets than their customers. In most cases, appeal after appeal drags on, and along the way the disgruntled customers drop their cases in the face of mounting legal bills. Sometimes a group of homeowners think they have a better chance by banding together and filing a class action suit against the builder. Unfortunately, the outcome is often not much different.

In the alternative, you may want to remove the binding arbitration clause from the contract. It will not eliminate the possibility of the arbitration as an option, just remove the exclusivity of it. Just know that it can serve as a tool to resolve disputes.

A one-way binding arbitration clause used by some builders binds the homeowner but not the builder to the decision of the arbitrator. NEVER agree to such a clause.

Other Contract Points:

Cost Overruns

Depending on the size of the builder, your exposure for cost overruns varies. Most, if not all large builders have firm pricing. With firm contract pricing you are insulated from cost increases that the builder may incur. In other words, if the total cost of drywall goes up by $400 after you sign the contract, the builder takes the hit, not you. This level of predictability is one of the benefits of dealing with a large, production home builder. In dealing with a smaller builder, custom builder, or you as general contractor, the cost will be passed on to you.

Design Changes

It is important to understand the motivations of the production builder vs. the custom builder. The large, production builder is concerned with streamlining the design and delivery of the product (your house). They want to eliminate variations in the process so they can increase speed, decrease errors, and increase profits. The custom builder looks to make money by, what else, customizing.

Production Builders

As part of the streamlining process, production builders have set floor plans that they offer in certain communities. They will allow you to choose colors and options before construction begins, but once your selections are made, they are pretty well set in stone. Production builders make it prohibitively expensive for you to make changes once construction begins because those changes, no matter how small, cost them money. The costs arise from the mistakes that can happen as the change makes its way through the chain of command or from the interest charged as a result of increased building time. Production builders usually don't hide the prices they charge for change orders, but make sure you have them in writing.

Custom Builders

In contrast to production builders, custom builders love to make changes! Want to move that wall? Sure! Just sign this change order and I'll collect the money later. If you are building a custom home, it is understood that changes will take place during the building process. The difference is that custom builders are aware ahead of time that changes will be made, so they adjust their price to reflect this fact.

Knowing When Your New Home Will Be Ready

One of the most nerve-racking experiences of buying a new home is selling your old one at the right time. Most builders will at least estimate a completion date, but very few guarantee it. Some larger builders will guarantee a date -- for a price. Here are some scenarios and suggestions on how to protect yourself:

Your new home is not ready in time

You can protect yourself against the risk of an unfinished home by having the builder at least guarantee a time frame when the home will be complete. A builder that can clearly lay out a schedule for you has a better understanding of the building process and has more control over their operation. Some builders will even guarantee a date when the home will be complete for an extra charge that may be included or added to the cost of the home. If a guarantee is not common in the area you are considering building, don't hesitate to have the builder create a milestone schedule that he is willing to guarantee. The milestone schedule can force him to commit to key dates when certain activities will be complete, such as foundation or framing.

Your new home is ready too soon

Believe it or not, this is a possibility. More and more builders are implementing "cycle time reduction" plans that cut down on the production time of the home. You need to plan in contingencies in the sales contract that will delay your closing until your current home is sold. Builders vary widely on this point. Some builders will buy your current home at a predetermined price if it does not sell before your new one is ready. This "Guaranteed Sales" program is great, as long as the predetermined price is not a "fire-sale" price. Other builders will not even begin construction if you have contingencies that include the sale of your existing home.

Whichever circumstance you are concerned about, addendums can be added to the purchase contract to protect you. Just ask your attorney to draft the language.

www.HOMEBUILDINGPITFALLS.com

HomeBuilding
PITFALLS

Chapter Eleven:

Understanding the Warranty

Let me get right to the point. The warranties of many big builders protect them, not you.

Things will go wrong with your new home. It's inevitable. The question is: Who is responsible for fixing these problems? All of this information should be spelled out in the builder's warranty. The builder's warranty is one of the items that you must read and understand before you make a buying decision. If the warranty references another document, such as standards set forth by a building trade organization or the state, make sure you also read and understand those documents.

The way the warranty reads will give you insight into how the company operates and the faith that they have in their product. Large builders usually have a more detailed warranty chock full of legalese, disclaimers, and limitations. Because the warranty is almost always referenced in the purchase agreement, it is a legally binding document that you are agreeing to, so make sure your attorney reviews it.

Industry Insight: *"We do that, but it's not written anywhere."*

Most production builders have a service department responsible for warranty work on homes. Very often, the service technicians will go outside the scope of the builder's warranty to please a customer. I had an experience with a builder that would often perform non-warranted work on customer's homes in the name of "customer satisfaction." Unfortunately, the generosity of the service technicians grew more costly and the company was nearly bankrupted. There was enough money, though, to pay for a warranty company to honor the warranties on some of the homes. The homeowners got a big surprise when they realized just how "limited" their "limited" warranty really was. The warranty company stuck to the letter of the warranty (instead of doing more than the warranty required like the builder had), resulting in a large number of angry customers. Remember, your warranty is only what is in writing and only as good as the company behind it.

You should compare warranties, tolerances, and remedies for different builders. If you have a huge crack in your garage floor, for example, is the builder's remedy to fill the crack with caulk or replace the floor? If the builder is informing you in writing before you even agree to buy the home that they are not going to stand by their product and fix something, that should send up a red flag!

Warranties vary greatly depending on the size of the builder and the area of the country. Some builders operate under a standard warranty that is mandated by the county or state government similar to a building code. The length of the different parts of the warranty will vary, just like new car warranties. Like a new car, you will have a responsibility to maintain your home to keep the warranty enforceable on the components in your home. For instance, is the concrete warranty void unless you seal your concrete? Remember, it's just like the warranty on a new car: If you don't change your oil as prescribed, kiss your warranty goodbye.

Most new home warranties have two components with varying terms of coverage. When you are shopping for homes you will commonly see "1-10" or "2-10" warranties.

One- and Two-Year Warranty Coverage

Think of this as the "Bumper-to-Bumper" version of your warranty. Almost everything in your home will fall under this category. From your squeaky floors to your doors that won't shut, it is the builder's responsibility to fix them for the period outlined in the warranty. Some builders will limit this part of the warranty to the major components of your home such as plumbing, heating and cooling, and electrical systems. Don't make the mistake of thinking absolutely everything (like caulk and paint) is covered. Read the warranty and all of its exclusions.

Structural Warranties

The longest period in most warranties offered by builders of new homes is the "Structural Warranty." This is the "10" in the "2-10" warranty. Think of this as the "drive-train" portion of your home warranty. Just as a new car warranty defines the drive-train warranty as covering just the systems that make the wheels move, the builder limits the Structural Warranty to the components that keep the home from collapsing. Structural defects usually refer to defects in the load-bearing portions of your home such as roof rafters or trusses, floor joists, beams, foundation, and footings. The structural portion of a warranty is not often invoked because, as most warranties read, the home must be deemed "unsafe for habitation" before the builder has a duty to repair the condition.

Industry Insight: *Third Party Warranty Companies* ♦WWW♦

Some builders handle warranty claims with "in-house" warranty employees who make service calls. Most big builder service technicians carry around a ladder and a tube of caulk and attempt to address the problems in new homes. Other builders rely on an outside company to handle warranty claims. Most outside warranty companies don't even have a ladder or a tube of caulk and you will never see them at your house. Instead, outside warranty companies offering "2-10" coverage simply act as a mediator between you and the builder.

I remember handling claims from a third-party warranty company. The company I worked for (which was close to bankruptcy) would get notices from the warranty company with copies of complaint letters from the homeowner. The letters would ask that the builder respond to the homeowner's problems. And that was it. Nobody from the warranty company assessed the problem at the home or made any attempt to fix it.

Items Almost Never Covered

From the time you move in, most builders will not warrant items such as landscaping, paint, caulk, floor coverings including carpet, vinyl, tile, and hardwood. You need to pay special attention to these, and any other items not warranted by the builder, during your walk-through. It is important to make sure the house is clean when you do your walk-through so that you can identify defects in any of these products and have them repaired prior to closing.

Manufacturers Warranties

Almost every component in your house has a warranty from the manufacturer. However, it is a bit unrealistic to think you are going to get the warranty card for the subfloor or concrete. What you should get is warranties from all of the major mechanical component manufacturers used in your home. Specifically, make sure you get the warranty information for:

- appliances
- garbage disposal
- furnace
- air conditioner
- water heater
- water softener
- windows
- entry doors
- garage doors and openers
- roofing material
- skylights
- whirlpool type tubs

If the builder uses name brand components with strong warranties you are protected even after the builder's warranty expires. In the case of a stove, there is little a builder can do to improperly install it and void the warranty. On the other hand, for something like a window or door, it is very easy for the builder to void the warranty by not installing it according to manufacturers instructions. If you do have a problem with the windows or doors several years after the builder's warranty expires, your claim could be rejected because the window or door manufacturer will simply say that the builder voided your warranty. If your windows carry a ten-year warranty and you have a problem (caused by your builder) in year seven, good luck going after the builder. Most builders look at a seven-year-old house as ancient and probably built in a neighborhood that was long ago completed.

So what can you do to protect yourself? First, make sure that your inspector is familiar with the components that your builder is using and can verify that those components are installed correctly. Second, you need to collect as much product information from the builder as you can, including warranty cards, installation instructions, and care and maintenance guides. Tell your builder that you are expecting these items to be given to you at the walk-through (new home orientation when the home is finished, but before closing). This is helpful if, for example, a builder tells you that the finish on your hardwood floor is not guaranteed by the builder, but it does carry a ten-year warranty from the manufacturer. Do you know who manufactured the floor? Do you know who installed it? Do you know how to care for it so as not to void the warranty? Does the floor really even have a warranty or is the builder just blowing smoke?

To curtail this risk, have a simple contingency or addendum added to your purchase contract stating that any warranty voided by the improper installation of any part or system used in your home will be the responsibility of the builder.

Your most serious warranty claims will stem from foundation and framing problems. If you verify that the foundation and framing are done correctly and products such as windows and doors are installed correctly, who cares how long your warranty is? No piece of paper or warranty company will take the place of a well-built house.

www.HOMEBUILDINGPITFALLS.com

HomeBuilding
PITFALLS

Chapter Twelve:

Knowing Your Supervisor's Experience

While the company you have contracted to build your home may have a solid reputation, it is the job supervisor or superintendent with direct control over your job who makes the most difference. Get to know this person before you sign the purchase agreement. You should have confidence that he or she will make sure you get a good house.

There are many ways to hide a builder's lack of experience in the home-building industry.

With over 20 years of combined experience in building homes...

That sounds good, but if there are six brothers in business, the phrase *"combined experience"* suddenly doesn't mean as much.

We have been building homes for over 50 years

Yeah, but when you meet the supervisor of the neighborhood you are considering, you find out he's only 21 years old! You know the saying: A chain is only as strong as its weakest link. This is a prime example.

Interview The Job Supervisor

There are some good questions you can ask a Job Supervisor/Superintendent to find out how well they know their stuff. Remember, it is this person's job to make sure that your house gets built on time, within budget, and with quality. As a rule, these are not people who have infinite knowledge about every aspect of construction. These are people who should be experts in organization, communication, planning, and scheduling. They need to be able to coordinate the "experts" who are performing the work. Here are some questions to gauge a supervisor's capability and background:

- *What is your background? Construction, Business...?* This drives the question: Did they just finish a career in used car sales? The ideal job superintendent would be able to communicate well not just with you but also with the subcontractors ("subs") actually doing the work. I have worked with those who could "schmooze" the customer but were not respected by the subs. I have also worked with superintendents who spoke in broken English but had a great deal of construction knowledge.

While you may be tempted into thinking, "I'll take the guy who I can't communicate with but knows a lot about construction." That is not always a good choice. The supervisor needs to understand your needs, desires, and wants and then clearly communicate them to the people actually performing the work. You will know if he communicates well with customers by asking current homeowners how responsive he was and know how well he manages subcontractors by how well the homes go together.

- *How many jobs (houses) are you responsible for?* This drives the question: What kind of attention can you give to my home? In a strong economy or a "hot" subdivision, a supervisor can be stretched thin. While no rule of thumb applies, he needs to be able to visit your house at least once a day. Ask the supervisor how many times a day he visits each job site. If all of his jobs are located within the same community, he can usually handle more work. If he is stretched between several communities, chances are he won't be available to actively manage the construction of your house.

- *What tools (scheduling software, etc.) do you use to manage your houses?* This drives the question: How organized will the process itself be? The more sophisticated builders analyze the entire building process and utilize tools to help the supervisor manage his jobs. Ask the builder if the scheduling tools he is provided with actually save him time or are just more paperwork.

- *What kind of training did the builder provide for you?* This drives the issue: How sophisticated is the company? Simple learn-as-you-go training is fine, but a formal education program shows that the company emphasizes education and quality.

- *How many assistants do you have and what are their roles?* This drives the question: Will you really be dealing with this person or one of their flunkies? Sometimes the person you are introduced to as being responsible for your home's construction is in fact not. Most large builders have supervisors with a number of assistants who play various roles in the construction of your home.

If a supervisor tells you they were a framer for 15 years before they got into supervising, that does not make them a good planner or scheduler. Likewise, if they say they worked in a similar position in a different industry, they may not cut it in the construction field.

Working for a larger builder with multiple communities in a city, it was easy to see how important the job supervisor's role is. Mind you, I worked for a production builder. Identical floor plans built in two different locations are supposed to be identical in design and quality, but that was not the case. The field supervisor had such a great effect on the final product that it would blow your mind. That is why it's important to talk to the homeowners in the community where you are looking to buy. Quality can differ from community to community, even with the same homebuilding company, because of the supervisor in charge.

Industry Insight: *From the Supervisor's Point of View*
By not arguing with the supervisor over little things, you can save your energy for the disputes that may arise over more significant defects. By not getting "under the supervisor's skin," constantly addressing the minor

issues, he will probably be much more receptive to addressing your concerns about the larger issues in a timely manner. Remember, the supervisor has more effect on the ultimate quality of your home than any other person. A little kindness with this person can sometimes go a long way.

Now, you may think that since you are paying a large amount of money for your new home, that you should be able to talk to your builder as much as you want, and that you should be able to address as many issues as you want, and that the builder should be working night and day to make sure that every square centimeter of your home is as perfect as it would be if it were built for a king and queen. Well, you absolutely have the right to get what you paid for. But you need to realize that your builder's supervisors are people, too. They only have a certain number of hours in a day to work. They want to spend time with their family in the evening just like everyone else. Although unfortunate, the reality at a large homebuilding company is that construction supervisors are frequently under great pressure to build as many homes in the shortest possible time. Therefore, the more time you spend talking to them, the less time they have to get their job done.

Having a "lame duck" supervise the construction of your home is another problem. In this scenario, the supervisor has already put in his notice to quit the company, but is still working for several more weeks. Mentally, this person has already left. He quits scheduling and supervising the subcontractors who will be building your home. Before you know it, your home is weeks behind, and there is little that the replacement supervisor can do to get you back on schedule. This situation is more common in a tight labor market where supervisors hop from one company to the next chasing the best offer. Hopefully, even if your supervisor is quitting, he will be mature enough to keep working on your home until his replacement arrives. The supervisor you are working with, just as any employee, could leave at any time, so it is important that any agreements you have are with the company he works for and not him as an individual. If you ask the supervisor to have the house cleaned up for your inspector's visits, you don't need to have it in writing. On the other hand, if your inspector discovers a major structural defect, don't just take the supervisor's word for it that he'll "take care of it next week." Get it in writing a signed by an authorized employee of the company.

HomeBuilding
PITFALLS

Chapter Thirteen:

The Home Inspector Scam

One of the best ways to make sure you get a quality new home is to have inspections done at key stages by a qualified inspector:

1. _Foundation_: to identify problems with the soil or the concrete foundation and to verify size and location of footers.

2. _Framing and Mechanicals_: a single inspection after the house is framed and mechanical systems (heating, cooling, plumbing, electrical) are installed. The idea is to inspect the structural integrity of the framing and the

condition of the mechanical systems before the walls are enclosed by drywall.

3. _Finish_: to inspect the home in its entirety, including the finished exterior surfaces and to inspect the installation of interior finish products.

Choosing an inspector can be a problem. The home inspection business has grown at a greater pace than even the homebuilding business itself over the past decade, resulting in a large supply of unqualified inspectors.

Most home inspectors in this country are unlicensed. National associations such as the American Society of Home Inspectors (ASHI) offer training and guidelines for member inspectors, but membership does not equal competence. Upon completion of a vocational school course or home study, you too can be a "certified" home inspector. Do not mistake an association membership with any type of license.

I have dealt with architects, engineers, and private building consultants on troubleshooting home construction problems. These people are not cheap, but they are the people I would want inspecting a home for me. You don't need a national expert, but in my experience, hiring local a registered architect dramatically increases your chances of getting a quality inspection.

Industry Insight: *The Role of an Architect*
The role of an architect is a unique one in the homebuilding process. The architect is the only professional to have a hand in the total design of the home. The design is not just the aesthetics of the home but more importantly the "system" of how the home will be constructed. The architect is trained to create a structure that melds hundreds of products and designs so that every component, when combined, will work in

> harmony. When you have a home built for you by a production builder, an architect designed it. Almost every building failure I have seen was because plans specified in the original design were not executed. When you hire an architect to oversee the construction of your home, it will be to verify that the home is built as designed.

The advantage that a traditional home inspector has over an architect is the inspector likely has more experience in evaluating the life expectancy of furnaces, water heaters, air conditioners, and appliances. But this ability is less important in a new home because all of those units are new and warranted by the manufacturer.

To take advantage of the growing demand for home inspectors, some companies began franchising home inspection businesses. Interestingly, any prospective inspector can give several thousand dollars to one of these franchisers, go through some training on how to run the business, and presto, they're home inspectors!

When I clicked onto a few of the franchise home inspection company Web sites, it appeared to me that the main objective was not to provide the potential home ʼbuyer with a quality inspection, but rather to sell franchises. Almost all of the franchise sites I have visited prominently advertise how easy it is to start their home inspection business. If you want even more examples of home inspection franchises, check out the list on Yahoo! ♦**WWW**♦

As part of the research for this book, I investigated one of the largest franchisers of home inspection companies. I visited their headquarters posing as a potential franchisee and listened to their sales pitch. I got the feeling they were trying to sell me not just on the merits of their franchise over any other franchise home inspection company, but also over all other franchises. The sad reality is that certain people who are interested in a franchise home inspection business are also considering opening some other type of franchise, such as a sandwich shop or a carpet cleaning business. They are not building professionals looking for a business opportunity. They are potential entrepreneurs who are deciding between making a submarine sandwich and conducting a home inspection.

When I worked for a large production builder, the majority of our customers who had inspections done on their homes used a typical home inspector -- not an architect, engineer, or even a former builder. As is so common, they came recommended from a real estate agent. I suggest you look elsewhere for a qualified inspector.

Industry Insight: *Home Inspectors and Real Estate Agents -- So Happy Together!*
The typical home inspector gets the majority of their business from real estate agent referrals. There is incentive for the inspector not to find too many construction defects and blow the deal for the agent, because if the sale goes through the inspector will have the opportunity for another referral from the agent in the future.

So you have a pretty good idea of who to avoid. Now how do you find a qualified individual to evaluate your new home? National organizations of qualified building professionals exist, such the American Institute of Architects (AIA), which has a great searchable Web site for residential architects at www.aia.org/consumer/. Simply search by state and then city, specifying "residential single family, all services." Look for a smaller firm, maybe even an individual who would be willing to take on a smaller scale inspection like this. Whatever the size of the firm, make sure the architect you choose has Errors and Omissions (E&O) insurance. E & O protects them (and you) in the event that they make a costly mistake. If you are having trouble finding an architect on the Web site, try calling your local AIA office. Larger cities have a local AIA office located in the business section of the Yellow Pages. ♦**WWW**♦

When contacting an architect or the AIA, describe your situation. Tell them you are building a home and would like an alternative to a traditional home inspector to evaluate your home at several different stages (foundation, framing/mechanicals, and finish as explained above). You want them to verify that the home is code compliant, using materials (described in the purchase agreement) that were installed according to manufacturer recommendations. Some architects have construction management and consulting experience, so they may know what you want. Some of the architects I talked with said that they do not have checklists and reports like a franchise home inspector does. Let them know that this does not concern you. You are not looking for a checklist, but rather a qualified individual to ensure that you are getting a well-built house.

You need to give your architect a plot plan, blueprints, materials list, and a schedule. You will need to coordinate the builder's schedule with architects to make at least the three visits mentioned. Never let a builder tell you they can't accommodate your request for inspections throughout the building process. Ask your architect to take photographs of any problems he or she sees on the job site. This will make it easier to bring the problems to the attention of the builder. It will also provide evidence and bargaining power if things go sour.

For the multiple visits, you will be expected to pay for the travel time of the architect and the time it takes him or her to document what they have observed and to make recommendations. Depending on the area of the country, you should expect to pay rates a little less than an attorney, so in the $100-an-hour range. You can try to negotiate a set price for the entire project or a cap on the cost to keep things under control. But if you spend $1,000-$1,500 on an architect, it will be the smartest money you spend on the entire project.

The Municipal Inspectors

So what role does the city or county building inspector play in all of this? Although some inspectors are dedicated and competent, others are lazy and in some cases even reckless. If they miss something during the inspection, no matter how obvious, they are usually not held responsible. In talking with the chief building inspectors in one of the fastest-growing cities in the country, I got the "lowdown" on their legal liability. As a government employee, neither the inspector nor the city will normally be held liable as long as the inspector is acting within their assigned duties -- even if they are negligent! The chief building inspector I was speaking with used this example: An inspector can visit a home under construction to perform an electrical inspection. He can completely botch the inspection, missing something that eventually causes a fire. But there may be little or no legal recourse for the home buyer because the inspector was acting (however incompetently) within his assigned duties. If, however, during an inspection he throws a hammer out a window and kills someone, he (and probably the city as well) will be found liable because it is not reasonable for an inspector to throw hammers through windows as part of his job.

It is also the responsibility of the municipal inspector to interpret the code. But what if their interpretation is wrong and later results in damage to a home or to injury to the home's occupants? Sorry, not much you can do. Again, interpretation is one of their assigned duties. Ultimate determination of liability and degree of responsibility are case by case and you should speak with your attorney about the level of government immunity in your community.

Industry Insight: *Breakin' 'Em In*

Your builder will focus on the items that will ensure that the home passes the needed inspections. Here is a little insight into what happens in the real world of municipal building inspections: When I worked for a large builder, whenever we would begin construction of home in a new jurisdiction, we would be "broken in" by the local inspectors. The inspector would fail us on repeated inspections (framing, plumbing, electrical, etc.). We quickly learned what exactly the inspector was going to be looking for during subsequent inspections. Every municipality would have inspectors who would focus more on certain areas and interpretations of the building code, and less on others. It was difficult for the inspector or the supervisor to make sure that every aspect of the house was code compliant.

It is one thing to strictly enforce one area of the code but not another; it is another thing to do a "drive-by" inspection. I remember a certain inspector was notorious for the "drive-by" inspection. There was no way he was going to get out of his car and get his boots all muddy even to perform something as critical as a foundation inspection!

Just as bad as incompetent and lazy inspectors are dishonest ones. There was a case of a municipal inspector who would offer to pass inspections on houses in exchange for materials for his personal use.

If you ask your builder to allow your architect or inspector to perform inspections for code compliance, you shouldn't get much resistance from the builder. Most if not all major construction problems can be avoided if homes are simply built to code.

Visiting the Job Site

If your schedule (and your stomach) allows it, visit the job site as frequently as possible. The more you are able to point out problems and mistakes and have them corrected *during* the building process, the smoother the entire process will be. But you want to make sure that you are welcome at the site. Your builder should have a program in place that allows for visits to the site with notice to the supervisor.

Scheduled Visits

In addition to a liberal visitation policy, the builder should have points in the building process where the homeowner, supervisor, (and sometimes the salesperson) walk the job site. These scheduled visits should take place at key times. (All of these will be expanded on in the chapters that follow). Key times are:

Before the lot is cleared: To discuss house placement on the lot, what natural features will be disturbed, and how the lot will eventually be graded

At the framing stage: To verify room dimensions, door and window locations, and to make sure floors, walls, and ceilings are plumb and square

At the mechanical stage: To verify plumbing, heating/cooling, and electrical outlets are in the correct locations before the walls are enclosed. Also check the location of exterior hose bibs (water faucets), lights, and electrical outlets

<u>At completion the "final walk-through"</u>: To demonstrate the operation of systems and appliances and to check for defects before closing

You can handle things like verifying locations of outlets so as to free up your architect for the more technical inspections. One of the best ways to protect yourself is to record on videotape or photograph the progress of construction. Countless times I have seen electrical outlets and vents covered over by drywall and floor coverings. On a much more important note, I can't stress enough how important it is to have the framing on video in case a structural issue comes about. Simply going room-to-room and documenting everything before drywall is installed can save you so many headaches down the road.

Surprise Visits
It should not be your intention to try to catch the builder doing something wrong. You should, however, make sure that the site is not in chaos on every day except for the day the builder knows you will be visiting. Remember the saying: Trust, but verify.

Knowing Who Is in Charge
If you visit your new home while it is under construction, you will more than likely find problems. You need to know who can address your concerns. Will it be the salesperson, the supervisor, or one of their assistants? Don't address the problem with just anyone on the job site; they may not have the authority to correct the problem.

More than likely you are not dealing with a one-man show. Your salesperson and job supervisor report to someone. You should know who these people are and how to contact them before a problem arises. If you are not getting results from the person you were told could handle your problem, you need to know where else to turn to resolve the issue.

HomeBuilding
PITFALLS

Chapter Fourteen:

The Building Process

If you have followed this guide's advice up to this point, your building experience will be much more pleasant. Just like building a quality home, you would have already built a solid foundation by doing your homework and communicating all of your concerns to your builder. If you were not able to follow the advice laid out in the earlier sections of this guide, either because you didn't have time or you were already too far into the process, don't worry; you can still protect yourself to some degree.

We don't need to go into complete detail about every step of the building process. Hundreds of activities in building a house take place at different stages. The activities can range from ordering the right amount of gravel to go around the foundation to installing the correct faucet in the hall bath. You don't need to know what needs to take place at every stage of the building process, but you do need to understand the basic order of how a house goes together.

The reality is that you have a job, a life, and a family. If you wanted to be a home builder, you would be doing just that. You just want a well-built home. My goal is to explain how to get that by concentrating on several key stages.

1. Lot Clearing and Excavation
2. Framing
3. Mechanical
4. Interior/Exterior at 90 Percent
5. Final Walk-Through

In keeping with the theme of the book, we want to concentrate on the choices in the building process that are the most difficult to change after closing. Choosing the wrong community or lot is much worse than having a bad drywall or paint job! That's why I stress engaging a qualified inspector at the early stages of construction of your home (foundation and mechanicals) rather than when most inspectors show up (a day before your closing).

At each of these stages either you or your inspector need evaluate certain activities or components that will be too difficult to explain in this book. But one thing is certain: you will need to be able to trust the builder and the subs working on the house. Once you trust, you need to verify.

You will be able to catch mistakes if you know what you are looking for. If the mistakes are caught early enough in the process, you can save everyone a great deal of headache. The reality is that you will not be able to check everybody's work. You can't be on the job site at all times. Even if you were, you probably wouldn't know if certain things were wrong. Would you know if a GFCI outlet was wired incorrectly or the truss layout what the architect specified?

As mentioned in the introduction, the ideal home-building experience would start with an informed buyer choosing a trusted, established builder. That builder would employ a competent supervisor who effectively schedules qualified subcontractors. An honest and knowledgeable inspector would inspect the work performed. Turn any of those positives into negatives and the result is a less than ideal building experience.

Clearing the Lot

The way the house is oriented on a lot will determine which physical features will remain intact after construction is complete. When you are dealing with smaller lots (less than an acre) expect that most of the lot will be disturbed during the construction process.

Before you or your builder can make any decisions about the lot, you need to have an accurate survey of the property. The survey will result in a plot plan showing your lot boundaries, setbacks, utilities, and natural features, including lakes and streams. To protect yourself, you may want to have a survey done by an independent survey company (in addition to the one done by the builder). This is especially important if you plan on putting up a fence or play equipment near the property line.

The first step in preparing your lot for construction is the clearing of earth. This involves removing trees, brush, and topsoil from the site. It is obvious why the trees and brush located in the area where the house will sit (called the building pad) need to be removed, but you need to discuss with your builder how much of the lot needs to be cleared and what vegetation and topography or physical features will be preserved. If your house will have a basement, the lot will need to be disturbed about ten feet beyond your building footprint to allow for over-dig and access to the bottom of the hole. The footprint of your home is a two-dimensional drawing of the first floor of your home. When you superimpose that outline on your plot plan, you can get an idea of what area of the lot will be disturbed. If your house will be constructed on a site that was a cornfield, the real concern is not the preservation of features, but rather the condition of the soil under the foundation.

Helpful Hints:

- Be sure to flag with bright ribbon or caution tape any trees or areas that your builder has agreed not to disturb during construction. Take pictures of the lot after the protected areas have been marked in case the flags or markers are removed.
- Include in your contract that the protected areas are included features of the lot that you are purchasing. If disturbed, you need to be compensated. You don't want the fifty-foot oak tree you fell in love with destroyed by a bulldozer before you move in and have a chance to enjoy it.

Staking the Lot

Depending on the size of your lot, you may not have much choice on the positioning of the home. Many developers create lot dimensions based on the minimum setback requirements defined by the municipality.

Setbacks:
- Front: the minimum or maximum distance that the home can be located from front of the lot, sidewalk, curb, or street.
- Rear: the minimum or maximum that the home can be located away from the rear lot line or easement. The rear of the home may or may not include any outlying structures such as decks, storage sheds, or play structures.
- Side yard: can be either a single measurement dictating the minimum distance from the side lot line or can be cumulative. An example is a 20' side yard requirement with a minimum of 5' on either side. This means that the homes cannot be constructed any closer than 5' together and that the distance on the opposite side must be greater than 15'. This allows some freedom in the placement of a side-entry garage, for instance. Be aware, your driveway is usually considered part of the calculation.

Regardless of the size of the lot and the home, the lot will need to be marked with stakes to show the footprint of the home. A mistake here can be a nightmare. You do not need to be a surveyor to see that something is wrong. Surveyors are human, and although they use a number of high-tech tools, they make mistakes. If it looks like the placement of the basement, footers, or foundation is much different than surrounding homes, question it.

Industry Insight: *Oops, I think we messed up!*
There are plenty of scenarios showing how a home can be "mis-placed" on a lot. I have seen homes built too close to each other because a builder relied completely on the stakes placed in the ground by the surveyor. In one case, the lot was oddly shaped, but the stakes clearly showed the rear corner way too close to the neighboring house. While construction continued, the neighbor who

---

had questioned the placement of the home finally got a survey to prove that the new home was outside of the setback line and on his property. The house under construction was now too far along to be moved. The builder ended up having to appear before several appeal boards and paying damages to the adjoining neighbor to pacify him.

I have also seen cases where a home is placed too far forward or back in the lot. The same regulations as above govern this "mis-placed" home. The problem in this case was that these homes were in the middle of a row of houses and were noticeably out of place. So, don't assume the survey and stake locations are correct. If something looks wrong, verify it and speak-up.

Setting Grade

Once you are confident that the house will be built in the correct location on the lot, you need to understand how high the house will sit on the lot. A mistake here can be a costly one for both you and the builder. The way the house sits on a lot can affect:

- drainage
- pitch of driveway
- usefulness of the lot
- appearance from the street
- sewer connection

The biggest issue is drainage -- both for the water runoff and sewer placement. If your house sits too low on the lot (i.e. the hole for your foundation is dug too deep), especially in relation to your neighbors, storm water run-off will flow down toward your house. Even if you don't have a basement to worry about flooding, your lot can turn into a swamp if there is not proper fall (or slope away) and a storm water management plan. Water management must begin early; it is usually not something that can be corrected later. If the top of your foundation wall will not be as high as your neighbor's, make sure there is enough space between houses to create a swale ("V" shaped channel graded to divert water) for drainage. The builder also needs to be aware of the sewer location because most all sewers work on gravity. Therefore, the connection to the house must be at the right level (i.e. the pipe must connect to the house at a higher elevation than where it connects to the sewer line in the street).

After the lot is cleared, but before the foundation is dug, the decision on the depth of the hole is made. For the purpose of this example, we'll assume the house has a basement, but the same calculation is used for a crawl space. The decision is made from several factors but is made by knowing what the height of the basement wall will be. A benchmark height marking the top of the basement wall, crawl space, or slab will be marked on a stake or tree so that the excavator can reference it. The hole depth is calculated by adding up the depth of the foundation and anything that will rest on top of it and then subtracting for the desired wall height above the current grade.

> *Example for calculating hole depth:*
>   basement wall- 8'
>   foundation- 1'
>   desired height above existing grade: 1'
>   (basement wall height + foundation depth)
>   – height above grade= 8' hole

Footing
The footing or foundation is the concrete slab or block on which the structure will rest. The walls of a basement will be poured or built on top of the footers. It is imperative that footers be constructed on solid ground. When it comes to the stability of

the ground under a foundation, the ideal is bedrock, the worst is sand. Some municipalities include a footer inspection as part of their standard inspection procedure. This inspection usually is limited to a visual assessment of the ground type and verification that the foundation is built correctly. If the foundation or soil inspection is not required, you or the builder may need to spend the money for a soil engineer to assess the quality of the ground. Your architect or inspector will be able to answer questions about unique soil conditions in your area.

In most developments, the earth is moved to create usable lots or pleasing topography. When this happens, some areas are excavated while others are filled. The fill area presents problems when it comes time to build if the ground is not properly compacted. This is not something you can identify on your own; leave it up to the experts.

Hillside developments present almost an expectation that movement will occur if the base of the hill is disturbed. Make sure you have an engineer (your architect can recommend one) review any special precautions taken due to poor soil conditions or hillside construction.

Helpful hints:

- Understand the soil conditions in the area. Leave it up to an expert to determine if the home you are considering can be built on the lot you have chosen.
- Have your architect verify the outline of the foundation or footer to check for square and to verify size.

Foundation Drainage

After the foundation is poured, perimeter drainage needs to be addressed. Even if you will have enough fall away from the house, you still need a drain system around the footer perimeter to divert water away from the foundation/basement walls. A typical footer drain system works by using a series of interconnected perforated pipes surrounded by gravel. This drain-tile (historically, it was actual tile used to drain surface water from farm land) is connected to a sump pump or exterior drain. If a sump pump will be used, the drain tile will be connected to a sump crock or well in the basement. The pump will sit in the well and expel the water to the outside of the house. The other way to handle the water from footer drainage is with gravity. If enough fall away from the property exists (such as with a walk-out basement), the footer can drain out a pipe at a grade lower than the foundation, such as down a hill. Whichever method is used, the idea is to provide an easy path for the water, decreasing the chance for water to enter your home.

Helpful Hints:

- If you have a sump pump, it is important to maintain it properly. If the pump becomes clogged, the sump crock or well will overflow and flood your basement.
- It is important to install a backup to your sump pump in case of power failure. This is a very common problem because the pump is most needed, coincidentally, when you are most likely to lose power -- during a storm.
- Do not use the electrical outlet provided for your sump pump for anything else. If the pump is sharing a circuit with a freezer, for example, you are more likely to blow a fuse and render your pump useless.
- Don't even think of finishing your home's lower level unless you know you have good drainage around your foundation. To be sure, allow your house to go through a full round of four seasons to test for water leaks and then you can be sure you have dry basement.

First Rough Plumbing

Before your lower-level concrete floor (basement or first floor) is poured, a rough plumbing installation will take place. If you have a basement, there won't be much to see, just the waste water lines. If you will have a rough-in for a bathroom in the basement, you will want to verify the location of the drains before the concrete floor is poured. If your concrete lower level is your first floor, all of your drains will be visible before your floor is poured. Again, you will want to verify the locations of both drains and water lines for sinks and toilets, because once the concrete is poured, it becomes a mess to move the plumbing lines.

Pour/Build of Basement/Crawl-Space Walls

If your home will have a basement, the walls will either be poured in place with concrete or built from concrete blocks. The basement/crawl-space walls will be constructed on the foundation. The width of the walls will depend on the material used (poured concrete or concrete block), the height of the wall, and the load each wall will have to bear.

You can learn more about concrete in Appendix B: Concrete.

Waterproofing and Pest Control

Before the excavated soil is filled in around your foundation, a waterproofing system needs to be applied to the walls. This does not serve as a complete barrier to water (even though it is commonly called waterproofing systems), but most applications help to seal the very porous concrete that comes in contact with the soil. Remember, your strongest line of defense against surface and ground water is good drainage. On the surface, that means proper grading away from the house, and at the foundation you need a good drain-tile system to get rid of ground water.

Pest control protection is also applied at this stage. The applications vary from area to area, but the most common are soil injections that help protect against termites.

Backfilling

After the foundation walls are complete, some of the earth that was excavated in order to build the foundation will need to be filled back in around the foundation. This "backfilling" as it is called, can put a lot of strain on the foundation walls. It is important that the walls have had a chance to cure. Your inspector will be able to give you an idea of how long the forms should stay on poured foundations because the cure time varies depending (among other things) on temperature and humidity.

Helpful Hints:

- Backfilling when the concrete is too "green" (not properly cured) and is not at full strength will cause problems with the concrete block or poured wall. Even if it is not evident immediately, the extreme force of the weight of the earth dumped back against the wall can be damaging in the future. The cure time for the concrete is dependent on a number of factors, with outside temperature being the most important. Large builders are notorious for pulling the forms off your foundation walls and backfilling too quickly.

- Remember, you need proper drainage away from the foundation to prevent surface water from exerting pressure against the foundation walls. If heavy clumps of clay or frozen earth are used in the backfill, several problems can occur. Sinkholes can form when either the clumps compress or when frozen ground defrosts and does the same. Imagine the clumps breaking down like ice cubes melting in a glass.

- Although the backfill may not represent the final grade of the yard, it needs to have the proper slope to allow water to easily flow away from the foundation.

Basement/ Garage Floors

The issues outlined in the concrete section can present themselves when you are pouring a concrete slab of any kind. You should apply similar practices to the concrete garage and basement floors.

It is important that the ground under a concrete slab be well-compacted using heavy machinery. Just like with the earth used to backfill the foundation, it is important that settling be avoided. The ground that the basement will be poured on was more than likely disturbed in order to excavate the site. If any filling of the area takes place, it is paramount that the ground is compacted or is filled with sand or gravel. When the concrete is cured it is like glass tabletop. The glass is strong, just as long as it is supported. The support for concrete comes from solid material below.

Framing

When it comes to framing a house, several methods can be used. Production home builders are often using techniques that more resemble manufacturing. Sometimes the lines are blurred between different types of builders.

Manufactured Home- What is commonly referred to as a mobile home

Modular Home- Home assembled in large, pre-finished sections

Panel Built Home- Sections pre-framed off-site then assembled-on site

Stick Framed Home- Assembled on site, piece by piece

You can find a good description of the framing process through links on our Web site. ◆**WWW**◆

To build a typical framed wall, the lumber is assembled on the subfloor and tipped into place. In panelized building, the wall section is built in a similar manner but off site with the assistance of a machine. The machine is programmed with the dimensions of the wall section and includes openings for doors and windows. The appeal of panelized building lies in the cost savings that result from reduced labor and increased speed of construction.

The most important issue when dealing with any portion of your home that is built off-site is its compatibility with the rest of the house. If the wall panels are made to the correct dimensions, but the foundation walls are not, you have a problem. Concrete foundations are not easy to change, so it is important that the dimensions of the foundation and walls are verified before framing begins.

Roof

The types of roofs used throughout the country vary. Regardless of which part of the country your home will be built, you need to have your inspector check two important areas of the roof. To prevent leaks, you need to make sure that intersections and penetrations in the roof are flashed correctly. Flashing is simply a way to integrate penetrations and intersections into the overlap or shingling of the roofing material. Another important area of concern is ventilation in a roof. By ventilating the roof, you are removing moisture that can build up in the attic. Trapped moisture will decrease the life of your roof. ◆**WWW**◆

You can learn more about the damaging affects of moisture throughout a home by reading the Moisture Section in Appendix A: Moisture.

Doors and Windows

The importance of flashing doesn't end on the roof. Anywhere rain can be deflected, flashing is needed.

Windows are typically secured in the framed opening using a nailing flange (an extension of the window used to secure it to the building) covered by an exterior cladding (brick, siding, stucco). Water can still get behind the cladding and the window if the window is not properly flashed. If flashing does not protect the framed opening, water can work behind the window into the wall cavity or into the house. If you have the luxury of watching the windows get installed, you will stop thinking of windows as protection from the elements but rather as just an extension of the "skin" on the house. Cladding needs to be an integral part of the window system. If the cladding fails, the window flashing should still provide some protection.

Industry Insight: *Security Systems Damage*

If you plan on having a security system installed, you need to know ahead of time what type of installation will be used. Of course, with any security system the idea is to detect intrusion from any door or window. That detection takes place by a sensor made up of contacts placed on the windows and doors. When these contacts separate, the alarm is tripped. The issue here is how the sensors are installed on the windows.

More than likely the sensors will need to be drilled into the window, either on the room side of the frame, or inside the window through the sill. If the sensor is installed on the room side of the sash, the screws that are used can penetrate the sealed area of the sash and cause the window to fail. If an adhesive is used to install the contacts, no damage is done to the window.

A more aesthetically pleasing installation of the security system contacts is to place the contacts inside the window where they are hidden when the window is closed. One part of the contact is attached to the lower sash and the other part is attached to the sill or frame. This can be the most intrusive installation and also the most damaging to the window. In order to hide the contacts and wiring, the installer usually drills holes through the sash, frame, and possibly the lower sill. That sill, with its drainage holes to the exterior, works as a last line of defense against water infiltration. If holes are drilled through the lower portion of the sill, new drainage holes are created -- right into the wall cavity! So instead of water being diverted to the exterior, water makes its way slowly into the wall. Water and walls don't mix well! I have witnessed the damaging affects of moisture trapped in wall cavities. Amazingly, the damage (including rot and mold growth) often goes unnoticed for years. For these reasons the warranty from most window manufacturers is voided if a holes are drilled into any part of the window.

The same precautions need to be observed with door installations as with windows. Most name-brand doors do not leak on their own. A leaky door is more likely the result of poor installation. Just like a window, a door is installed in a framed opening and surrounded on the exterior by either cladding or trim (casing). The door and the cladding are not the only line of protection against water infiltration. Flashing needs to be installed to protect the inside of the home against water that makes its way between the installed door frame and the framed opening of the home. Think of a door or window much like a skylight in a roof. Simply cutting a hole in a roof and placing in the skylight would certainly cause a leak unless special attention is paid to the flashing.

Housewraps

Housewraps are becoming more popular as an air barrier between the exterior sheathing and the cladding (such as siding or brick). Housewraps work by creating a continuous barrier that resists wind and rain. A properly installed housewrap should keep a house dry even before the cladding is installed. The most popular housewrap is Dupont's Tyvek®. Unfortunately, few contractors understand how to correctly install Tyvek® or any other housewrap. ◆**WWW**◆

The most important practice in installing any housewrap is to make sure the wrap is shingled properly. The Tyvek® Web site has great illustrations and videos of proper installation. An improperly installed housewrap can cause water infiltration problems, so have your architect check the installation of the wrap before the cladding is installed.

You should note that all housewraps are known as secondary moisture barriers. The primary moisture barrier is the cladding (siding, brick, etc.). Housewraps will not compensate for poor construction techniques. If your builder is using a moisture-absorbing cladding such as brick, a housewrap will not prevent moisture from passing through the wall if the required air space does not exist. (You will see why later in this chapter).

Rough HVAC: Heating, Ventilation, and Air-Conditioning

Whether your home has forced air heating/cooling, or radiant heat, the lines will be run through the floors and walls before the drywall is installed.

Forced air systems deliver conditioned air through a series of pipes or ducts to attain the desired room temperature. The air inside the home is recirculated through the home by returns that draw air from the home back to the heating/cooling unit. There are different variations on the air delivery/ return system.

Supply:
Floor vent air delivery: Preferred in climates where most of the system's use will be in heating the home. Because heat rises, it is a more efficient way of attaining the desired room temperature.

Ceiling vent air delivery: Delivers Heated/Cooled air through vents in the ceiling. This method is preferred in climates where the unit will primarily cool the space. It is also a less expensive method of air delivery because it is easier to run ductwork through the attic area than it is through the floors.

Return:
Room air return: In order for the air to recirculate in the home, it needs to be delivered back to the unit. A more balanced approach is to retrieve air from each of the rooms. This creates a more balanced system allowing for greater circulation of air.

Central air return: Instead of pulling air from each of the rooms, a less expensive alternative is to use a central return to pull air from a central area such as hallway. This can create a pressure imbalance, though, by delivering the newly conditioned air into a room and pulling the old air from another location.

Another method for heating the home is radiant heat. Historically, radiant heat followed the fireplace as the preferred method of heating. The system works by heating a liquid, usually water or glycol, and delivering it through pipes to rooms where the heat is released into the room. The heat can either be delivered by radiators or by snaking the lines under the floor and allowing the floor to heat the room.

Second Rough Plumbing Stage

Another activity that takes place while the walls are "open" is the second plumbing rough-in. It is called a rough-in because no finished fixtures will be installed yet. It is the second part of the rough because the first took place with the installation of plumbing pipes under the basement or first-floor concrete slab.

For all floors other than the basement or slab, the plumbing lines will be run up through the floors and behind the walls. If you have a blueprint, take your tape measure and verify the locations of hot, cold, and drain lines. There is some room for error during the first stage of rough plumbing (with the exception of toilet drains) because most lines can be adjusted to fit inside cabinets and under counters and sinks. But if the lines are off by more than a few inches, or they are missing completely, there will be some major problems after drywall is installed! Remember to mark additional plumbing options on your print and verify that they are present after the rough-in.

Helpful Hints:

Don't forget:
- icemaker line
- additional fixtures outside the home or in the garage
- basement or additional bathrooms
- laundry tubs

Rough Electric

At this stage, the wiring for outlets and fixtures will be run through the walls, just as the plumbing and HVAC has been. No fixtures will be installed at this point, but the boxes that the outlets and lights will be secured to will be. The phone, cable, security, home automation, audio, and video lines should all be run at this point also. Just as with the plumbing rough-in, you need to verify the location for the fixtures, outlets, and switches that will be installed later.

Helpful Hints:

- Make sure that all outlets, fixtures, telephones, audio, video, and security equipment are wired into the correct locations in each room
- Verify that light switches will not end up behind the door when it is opened and fixtures will be centered in the finished ceiling or in the locations that you want- (in the middle of a kitchen island, foyer, bedroom, hallway, or even a possible pool table!)

Exterior Cladding

You have many choices in deciding what will cover the outside of your house. However, There are special considerations for whatever system you or your builder chooses. Some cladding material blocks moisture completely (synthetic stucco) while others manage water by shedding (vinyl siding) still others absorb and then expel moisture (brick). The more complicated systems such as synthetic stucco (or Exterior Insulated Finish System) require a great deal of expertise. Here are some resources for different types of cladding:

EIFS - Exterior Insulated Finish System

If you are considering using a synthetic stucco system, your architect needs to be very familiar with the proper application of the system. This is not something to take lightly; I have seen firsthand some of the incredible damage that can be caused by what are called "barrier" systems. Barrier systems attempt to keep water out completely (which is very difficult) and can trap water behind walls. The opposite of a barrier system is a drainage system in which moisture that gets behind the cladding is allowed to escape. The National Association of Home Builders has a good basic overview of some of the problems with synthetic stucco. ♦**WWW**♦

Brick Veneer

Surprisingly, some of the same problems with stucco can also be caused by brick veneer if it is not installed correctly. When you drive through a modern neighborhood and see brick on a home, the brick likely serves no structural purpose, and hence is called a veneer. Brick is very porous and can absorb water like a sponge. If that water is not properly managed by ventilation and flashing, trapped moisture can cause mold growth and rot resulting in serious structural damage. With wood-framed houses, brick is installed as a veneer so that neither the brick nor the mortar comes into contact with the building. If you think of bricks and mortar as sponges, you understand why you need to keep an air space between the back of the brick and the exterior sheathing or housewrap. The Brick Institute of America has a very thorough overview of proper brick installation. ♦**WWW**♦

Siding

Vinyl siding is probably the least likely of all cladding materials to cause damage to your home. However, it can be installed incorrectly, causing it to appear wavy when it expands and contracts. Because vinyl expands and contracts, it needs to be hung on the building in a way that allows for movement. ♦**WWW**♦

Wood and fiber-cement board siding, like all cladding, can cause moisture damage if not properly installed. Installation information can be found through a link on our site. ♦**WWW**♦

Insulation

When all rough-ins are complete (HVAC, plumbing, electrical) it is time to insulate the walls. The method for insulating varies from region to region depending on the climate. Regardless of the climate, insulation works to maintain the desired interior temperature. The use of deeper 2X6 walls instead of 2X4 walls allows for more insulation in the exterior walls, but many builders do not want the added lumber and insulation costs.

Drywall

Now it is time to "close-up" the walls that have been open since framing began. The material of choice for most builders is drywall (Sheetrock, gypsum, or wallboard).

Sheets of drywall are secured to the studs with screws and nails. The joints are then taped and covered with several coats of drywall compound or "mud."

Hanging:
According to the leading drywall manufacturer, the recommended pattern of nailing is as follows:
Nailing: space nails a maximum of 7" apart on ceilings, 8" on walls, and at least 3/8" from ends and edges
Screwing: space screws a maximum of 12" apart on ceilings, 16" on walls, and at least 3/8" from ends and edges of panels. Sink screws to just below the panel surface, leaving the paper intact.

Taping:
The joints of the drywall need to be covered with mud and either paper or fiberglass mesh tape. If the joints were simply filled with drywall mud, cracks would begin to form wherever a void occurred. The tape, although not an adhesive, creates a continuous surface connecting all of the sheets of drywall.

Finish coats:
The joints, corners, nail and screw marks are all covered with drywall mud. Several coats of drywall mud need to be applied, allowing at least a day before the next coat is applied. Each coat covers a larger area so that the joint or nail hole is hidden and seams are blended in with the wall.

Sanding:
After all drywall compound has dried, it needs to be sanded. The joints are feathered out so they are not noticeable when they are painted. This is dusty procedure and not an activity you want to be around for! If you have ever been in a house after the drywall was sanded you know that the dust settles everywhere. The duct work should be covered to reduce the amount of dust settling in the HVAC system.

First Paint "Roll-out":
When the drywall is finished, the quality of the work cannot be seen completely until paint is applied. The first application to the walls and ceilings takes place just before the interior trim is installed. It is much easier to get a coat of paint on the walls before trim or any electrical or plumbing fixtures are installed.

The remaining steps in the construction process are all "finish stage" in nature- interior trim, cabinets, flooring, final electrical and plumbing, yard and landscaping. It is up to your trained eye to determine if these stages of work were correctly done. The formal review of all of these finishes and the demonstration of how all of the systems described above all work together takes place in your walk-through.

HomeBuilding
PITFALLS

Chapter Fifteen:

Walk-Through and Punch-Out

The walk-through, also known as a new home presentation or orientation, is your chance to review the final product delivered to you. You will be given the opportunity to document any problems (creating what is called a "Punch List") you have with the home and have them corrected before you close. If you have taken this book's recommendations throughout your building process, your walk-through should be a breeze. If not, major items that may be difficult to repair at this stage could appear and make your last step in the process a difficult one.

Another function of the walk-through is to learn about the operation and care of the home. Since this is a new home, you may not be familiar with some of the new features. It is the builder's role to explain them to you. Be sure to ask questions; it's the builder's job to know the answer. The reality is that he may not always know the right answer, so try to verify anything that may sound unreasonable. I was at a walk-through with a builder and a customer asked what was under the black cap in the basement floor. The builder told the customer it was a check valve (which was correct) that prevented any of the toilets in the home from overflowing (which is not correct). In this case, the check valve was installed to prevent sewage from surrounding homes from backing up into the lower level of the home.

There are some items the person conducting your walk-through must explain, show, or demonstrate to you.

- water shutoff(s): check for a main shutoff for the entire house's water supply. If a pipe ever breaks, you need to have easy access to the shutoff to stop the flow and prevent further damage.
- gas water heater or furnace pilot light: most furnaces now have an automatic pilot light but many gas water heaters do not. Have the builder demonstrate the proper lighting technique.
- sump pump dedicated electric line: if you have a sump pump it should be plugged into a dedicated outlet on its own circuit.
- proper electrical panel description: the electrical panel should be easy to access and each circuit/room properly labeled so that you can troubleshoot when a circuit breaker trips. The labels should be logical and legible.

Your walk-through should take place after your architect or inspector has completed a thorough inspection of the entire finished home and checked for the proper installation and operation of all the building components, code, and industry standard compliance. You should have a copy of the final report to use during the walk-through to review with the builder.

Before the walk-through, the home must be clean and 100 percent complete. If the home is not clean, it is difficult to identify damage to items such as cabinets and counter tops whose cosmetic condition may not be warranted after closing. If finish items (such as carpet or baseboards) are missing at the walk-through, the chance of damaging some other part of the home when they are installed increases, creating more delays and problems.

To cut down on confusion, bring along a copy of the contract, plans, specifications, options, selections, and change orders for the house. If a color or fixture is wrong, it is much easier to prove when you have documentation of what you ordered. If industry standards apply in the area, make sure you not only understand them, but also bring them along. This comes in handy when questions arise about when something such a crack in a concrete slab warrants repair or replacement.

Your walk-through should be conducted with the supervisor or person you have been dealing with up to this point. Sometimes builders use one of their service technicians or warranty representatives to perform the walk-through. If the supervisor who is familiar with you and the job is not present, the person conducting the walk-through may not be familiar with any ongoing issues you have had with the home. Moreover, you will be wasting time bringing that person up to speed. Having both the supervisor and the warranty representative (or whoever will be responsible for any warranty claims you have on the home after closing) present could be a benefit. It would be in the best interest of whoever handles your claims after closing to ensure that your home is in good shape before closing.

The builder may have performed dozens or even hundreds of walk-throughs, and may have a set routine. A routine is fine as long as it doesn't rush things along, make you uncomfortable, or place the balance of power in his hands. Don't let the builder dismiss your requests with comments like "We never do that," "That's as good as it gets," or "That's the way it's supposed to be." Remember, you should have already set the tone from day one in the building process: I am the customer, I have high expectations for the finished product, and I am going to protect myself to ensure that I get what I pay for. Do not allow the builder to bully you or pressure you into accepting a defect. If it's not right don't close.

> **Industry Insight: *"But we always do it that way."***
> The fact that a builder "always does it that way" is in no way reassurance that it is the right way to do it. This is especially dangerous when it comes to production builders because they repeat the same techniques on every home. I have seen production builders repeat a flawed construction technique hundreds of times resulting in literally millions of dollars in damage. It is one thing to make a mistake, but another thing to make the mistake part of your routine and repeat it hundreds of times.

If you are using a standardized "walk-through form" supplied by the builder that only has a few small lines to document the defects you find, forget about it! That is just a ploy to make it look like you should only have a few items that you need corrected or that the sheet is only for major problems that need to be addressed. I know of a builder who actually revised the walk-through form so that it had half as many preprinted lines to list items. Changing the form resulted in fewer items on each walk-through. If not many problems exist, great. But if many do exist, they need to be documented. You may need to use more than one form to list all of your "punch list" items or you can write "continued on page ___" on the original form and continue on another sheet.

Don't make any verbal agreements with the builder. If they really are going to do what they say, they shouldn't have any problem putting it in writing! Don't fall for any of their sob stories about how the supervisor will be fired if he has another punch list with a lot of items, etc. Oh, and one more thing -- no side lists. A side list is a list of items the builder agrees to do -- they just don't want them on the "official" punch list form. Remember that the punch list form you are using is a legal document. Any other side lists you create hold no more weight than a verbal agreement. Some builder's walk-through forms used to make punch lists actually contain language to the effect that no other agreements, verbal or written, have been made between you and the builder, or any of its employees or subcontractors. But you should know that because your attorney would have already reviewed it.

I can't stress enough how important it is to have the home complete before you close on the house and the builder gets its money. I have seen hundreds of cases where homeowners move into a home that "had just a few things" that needed to be completed. Well, those few things either took months to get done or were never completed at all. Just as important is never accepting a verbal agreement for work that needs to be completed after the walk-through. I have heard from HUNDREDS of homeowners who said someone "told me," "promised me," "swore to me" that "he was going to be back to fix it." When the person who made the promise is fired, quits, or moves to another community, you will be left holding the bag caught playing a game of he-said she-said.

It is critical not only to document every problem, but also to have in writing exactly what the builder will do to correct the problem. For example, see the big difference between:

Item 26 <u>Scratch in counter top right of kitchen sink</u>

and

Item 26 <u>Replace counter top due to scratch right of sink</u>

The first statement puts remedy of the problem at the discretion of the <u>builder</u>. The second statement clearly states <u>your</u> intended solution to the problem.

Remember that your walk-through is to identify major items that need to be addressed. Do not be overly concerned about slight paint or drywall imperfections. You need to see the forest through the trees. If your face is plastered against the wall trying to find an imperfection in paint, you may miss something bigger, like a floor out of level. If you have followed the advice in this book, you will undoubtedly have a reputation with the supervisor! The supervisor may not be used to the way that you are approaching the homebuilding process. While you may be known as the "picky customer," they need to understand you are only trying to protect yourself and to get what you paid for -- nothing more, nothing less. The supervisor should know and understand that.

Through the Walk-Through

You should check every room for the basics:

Floors:

Walk into the room and check the floor for any imperfections, squeaks, stains, or scratches. Each area of the country has different industry standards, so make sure you read and understand them before you begin the walk-through. For instance, some industry standards allow for visible seams but do not permit loose subflooring.

Carpeted areas should contain no visible color variations (regardless of what the industry standard says). Hardwood will expand and contract, showing gaps between boards, but the gaps should be consistent. Floor tile should not be chipped, gouged or scuffed. The grout should be a consistent color and not broken out anywhere. Vinyl flooring should be smooth without any visible seams or ridges from the underlayment.

Your builder should provide warranties for whatever floor coverings you have in your home. Just like all of the warranties you will be provided with, you need to activate your warranty by sending in the registration. If the builder uses good materials from reputable manufacturers, you will be protected long after your builder's warranty expires. For example, the largest manufacturer of hardwood flooring, Bruce, offers a lifetime warranty against buckling and various warranties on the finish. ♦**WWW**♦

Of course, to keep your warranty valid, you need to understand the proper care of the floor covering. Follow the manufacturer's recommendations rather than the builder's advice.

Walls and Ceilings:

As I mentioned, don't expect perfection in the condition of the paint and drywall in every room, but make sure that it is complete. If any touch-ups were made, they should be seamless and not draw your attention. Because of the way people view ceilings, touch ups are often very noticeable. A total re-paint is usually necessary. You will be hanging pictures and covering up walls, but most people don't do much to their ceilings, so insist that you want them done right.

Doors:

Doors should close properly with a consistent reveal, meaning that when the door is shut, it is centered in the door frame. The doors and their frames will swell and shrink with changes in humidity, so it is not uncommon for doors in new homes to need adjustment within the first year. Sliding doors should roll freely without binding. If you have a spring-loaded door, to your garage for instance, it should close itself from any position.

Switches and Plugs:

It is a good idea to bring along an outlet tester for the walk-through. They can be picked up for a few dollars at any hardware store. It makes it easy to run through a room and make sure every outlet works properly and ensure that the outlet is wired correctly. If a problem can be identified and corrected before closing, you will save the trouble of having an electrician cutting holes in your walls later. An electrical inspection is almost always required before your certificate of occupancy is issued in a home. But don't think that the inspector went around and checked every outlet. In bathrooms and wet areas, a GFCI outlet is required. If a wet area contains several outlets, it is possible that the outlets are all wired together. The electrical tester will allow you to "trip" the circuit, cutting off power to simulate something like a hair dryer falling into water.

If you do not have overhead light fixtures in a room, but instead have switched outlets, make sure that the outlets are wired correctly.

Ask your builder to correct things you find quirky. If a series of switches seem counterintuitive, ask that they be put in an order that makes sense to you. For example, when you walk into a room, the first switch should be for a light, not a ceiling or exhaust fan. Check that all three-way switches work properly and that each switch will operate regardless of the position of the other.

Windows:
As you go from room to room, check for the proper operation of each window. Moveable windows should hold their position when opened, tilt in with ease, and lock and unlock smoothly. If you have double-paned windows, there should not be any clouding or hazing between the panes. The windows need to be clean for the walk-through so that you can inspect the glass for any scratches.

Bathrooms:
Besides the usual floors, walls, ceiling, paint, electrical (pay special attention to electrical in the bathroom!), test the plumbing. Make sure that the hot water comes out of the hot side and cold out of the cold side of the faucets and showers. It sounds basic, but it can and does get mixed up. Water pressure should be strong enough that water shoots and not dribbles out of showerheads or faucets. If you have a whirlpool tub, fill it up and try it out! Flush the toilet and check for any leaks around the base or where the water closet meets the bowl. Run the faucets and check for any leaks under the vanities.

There are removable screens that can be unscrewed from the discharge or aerator of most faucets. This screen catches small particles inside the pipes, especially due to installation. Have your builder show you how to remove the aerator and clean the debris before you use the faucet.

Kitchens:

Just as in the bathroom, check the faucet for hot and cold water and leaks. Also check the operation of the garbage disposal with the water running. It is not at all unusual for construction debris to fall into the disposal during construction, so make sure that you hear no unusual sounds when the disposal is operating. Run the dishwasher through an entire cycle to check its operation and verify that it drains properly; you can just let it run while you walk through the rest of the house. Check each of the burners on the stove and turn on the oven. If you have an exhaust fan vented to the outside, make sure it really does force air out by turning on the unit and going outside to the discharge. Place a cup of coffee in the microwave and see if it works. Open all of the cabinets and drawers and make sure they look level and flush when they close. Really give that kitchen a workout!

Maintenance:

In addition to the safety demonstration mentioned above, the builder should also demonstrate normal maintenance such as caulking or changing air filter or cleaning the humidifier (on forced air systems) or how to drain sediments from your hot water tank. ♦**WWW**♦

Attic:

Your inspector will probably have a look at the underside of the roof after it has been framed, but he should be back up there for his final inspection to check for insulation and any signs of daylight (other than from ventilation).

Exterior:

Your inspector's final visit should include a thorough inspection of the exterior, including the roof. The key here is water management: from roof runoff, water runoff from adjoining property, etc. Ask your inspector to check the flashing details especially at roof intersections and penetrations. All exterior surfaces should be sealed wherever a penetration occurs, including from air conditioner lines, outlets, or electric meter.

www.HOMEBUILDINGPITFALLS.com

HomeBuilding
PITFALLS

Chapter Sixteen:

After You Close

You will have service issues after you close -- that is a guarantee. But who do you call? If you are expected to contact the subcontractor who performed the work (i.e. call the plumber for a plumbing leak) then you need a list of everyone who worked on the house. If you call the service department of the builder, find out how long they have to respond to your request and what you are to do in case of emergencies. Proper documentation means getting it in writing.

Document serious problems in writing. A door squeak is a minor problem; a roof leak is a big problem. Most warranties will be extended for as long as a documented ongoing problem occurs. The key is that it must be documented for it to have any teeth. Your call to the customer service or warranty department is not considered sufficient.

Here is a real-life case of how this can be a problem. A number of customers of a builder had problems that were addressed by the builder, but not fixed within the time of the warranty (in this case one year). The builder was then sold to another company. The new builder was aware of ongoing undocumented problems but played dumb and repeatedly responded by saying: "Sorry, you're out of warranty." Those people that did have documented ongoing problems received service because the new company recognized their liability because a paper trail had been started.

HomeBuilding
PITFALLS

Chapter Seventeen:

The Pitfall Chronicles

When I headed the warranty department for a large national production builder, I dealt with the angriest of customers across the country. Although I didn't directly have a hand in the cause of their complaint (I didn't build their home and the customer was often calling from a different part of the country), I represented the company that caused whatever problem they were facing. In this position, literally hundreds of letters from disgruntled homeowners would come across my desk. I remember one in particular that chronicled the last twelve months of a customer's life while building what was to be her "dream home." I thought I had seen and heard every complaint a customer could have had, but this letter was different. In ten pages, this woman chronicled almost every bad experience she had throughout the sale, construction, and service phases of the homebuilding process. To help provide a summary for this book, I think it is important to list chronologically some of the more common problems that can arise throughout the building process and some suggested solutions.

Pitfall:

The salesperson you are dealing with moves to another community. A new salesperson takes over negotiations and does not honor verbal agreements made with the previous salesperson.

Prevention:

As you progress through negotiations, you should put in writing everything that you and the salesperson agree on: deposit amount, included options, final sales price, etc. The salesperson (or any employee or company representative you are working with) could be fired the next day and you would have to start all over. Before you sign any purchase agreement or sales contract, your attorney should review all documents.

Pitfall:

You choose a beautiful lot that your salesperson told you borders a nature preserve. You are more comfortable paying the hefty "lot premium" because you think you will be able to get your money out of it if you sell your home. After moving in, you realize that your back yard does not, in fact, directly border the nature preserve. Instead, your lot borders a strip of land owned by a utility company that you are forbidden to cross to get to the nature preserve. To make matters worse, after living in the home for more than a year, the developer puts in a walking trail across a ten-foot wide easement that runs the length of your back property line. As the community grows, more and more residents take advantage of the walking trail and invade your privacy and enjoyment of the back yard you paid extra for because you thought your lot bordered a nature preserve and had no idea the easement could be used by the whole community.

Prevention:

You need to understand for what adjoining property can and can't be used. Never let a salesperson sell you a bill of goods by painting you an inaccurate picture. Your attorney or the planning and zoning department of the municipality can help you understand the permitted uses of adjoining property and any easements or encumbrances on your property. Remember, if you pick the wrong color for the front door, you can always repaint it. If you pick the wrong lot, you may be stuck.

Pitfall:

You are prevented from bringing in your own inspector early on, even though you had an addendum to your contract that you thought allowed access for your inspector at any time. Your builder shows you the standard "Inspection Addendum" you signed that clearly states that the home will only be made available to your inspector for a final inspection immediately prior to closing.

Prevention:

Make sure that your attorney reviews all "standard" forms used by the builder. Such addendums and contingencies may have hidden clauses that favor the builder. In this case, the addendum should have at least mentioned key inspection points.

Pitfall:

When you are out at the job site after work, you verbally notify the assistant construction supervisor about some major concerns you have about a wall that looks out of square. He assures you that he will address the issue but that it's really "not a big deal."

Prevention:

When you have problems throughout the process, they should be documented and addressed to the proper person. If you verbalize a problem to a person that has no authority to correct it, you are wasting your time. Make people on your "team" aware of problems and let them decide if they are a "big deal." For example, your attorney and not your salesperson should decide if a contractual issue is of concern. Likewise, your architect or inspector should decide if construction defects are major or minor.

Pitfall:

You are notified of the date of your final walk-through. You know that the home isn't ready but you show up for the walk-through anyway. The home is dirty and doesn't even have electricity yet.

Prevention:

Never allow the builder to force you into a walk-through until the home is finished and clean. You cannot assess the quality of the finished product if the home is not actually complete. If the home is dirty, you may miss scratches or gouges in counters or floors that certainly won't be covered after closing. Don't even bother performing a partial walk-through. Pressure the builder to reschedule.

Pitfall:

You go ahead with the walk-through and document as many problems as you can find. When you return several days later, the house is clean and most of the items from the list are complete. The problem is that in correcting some of the defects you documented, the builder caused more problems. For example, they replaced the defective dishwasher, but in doing so, damaged the hardwood floor in the kitchen. Also, in cleaning the house, more problems became apparent. There is no way they can correct all of these problems before your closing this afternoon!

Prevention:

Don't put yourself in a position where you are forced to accept sub-par work. Your attorney should have included in your contract language stating that you would not close until all outstanding items are complete. If that means pushing your closing off another two weeks and living in a hotel, then so be it. Once your builder gets his money, the bargaining position changes completely; they will care MUCH LESS about you and your home.

Pitfall:

You go to closing with the assurance from the supervisor and his boss that the items will be complete within a week of closing. Several weeks go by and some items remain unfinished. The biggest problem is that your air conditioner is blowing warm air. You are told to contact the heating and air contractor and set up a time to meet at your home. You take off work, but the contractor doesn't show. So you reschedule with the very apologetic contractor for next week. You take off time the following week and meet the contractor. He shows up this time, but without the right part. Guess what? More time off of work and more frustration. You are going on three weeks without air conditioning and you knew it didn't work before you went to closing.

Prevention:

Problems not resolved while the home is unoccupied only magnify after you move in. You may have to take time off from work, the contractor may not show up, the "fix" might just damage something else, only compounding the problem. Be sure to have <u>all</u> issues resolved before closing.

These scenarios are neither fictitious nor uncommon. I have dealt with customers who have faced much worse circumstances. I have spoken to new homeowners who wished a broken air conditioner was the worst of their problems. Imagine having to move out of your six-month-old home for three weeks so that major structural repairs can be corrected because of the utter incompetence of the framer and a municipal inspector who looked the other way. Imagine having to live in your two-year-old home while the synthetic stucco skin is removed and rotted wood replaced and toxic mold cleaned because of persistent, hidden leaks.

I hope that you have learned how critical some of the steps are, even before the first shovel of dirt is turned. Just like building a house, the process starts with a solid foundation of homework and protection. I truly hope my insights into the world of homebuilding have helped you to avoid the pitfalls of building a new home.

Appendix A: Moisture Problems

Bulk Water and Vapor Intrusion:
The Biggest Problems Facing New Homes

Many new homeowners have dealt with the problems of roof leaks, window leaks, plumbing leaks, and water in crawl spaces and basements. Sometimes, the damaging effect of moisture is not immediately noticeable. Recently I was fortunate to work on a project that allowed me to see inside the walls of over 100 newer homes in order to solve moisture problems. I have seen the destruction that water infiltration and water condensation can have on a home that may be less than a year old. Water can cause enormous problems, and unnoticed can create damage inside walls, crawl spaces, and attics.

Bulk Water vs. Water Vapor
The effects of moisture damage go beyond just rotted wood, damaged drywall, and interior surfaces. As houses are built more air tight in order to be more energy efficient, moisture, either in the form of vapor or liquid, cannot exit the home as quickly as it is introduced. Moisture in wall cavities, attics, basements, crawl spaces, and under floor coverings lingers, rotting wood and feeding mold that can be harmful to the health of the home's occupants.

Bulk Water

Bulk water can be introduced into the home from:

- roof leaks due to missing shingles, improper flashing of roof intersections such as valleys, or roof penetrations such as vents
- improperly installed windows and doors
- improperly flashed cladding (brick, siding, or synthetic stucco)
- ice dams formed under shingles and roof sheathing
- one-time or persistent plumbing leaks both from delivery and waste lines
- leaky basements or crawl spaces

Roofing materials such as wood, asphalt, or fiberglass shingles or roof tiles are not waterproof. They work by overlapping or shingling each other so that water is shed from the roof. The biggest problem with new roofs is not how the shingles or tiles are applied but what happens when the two sections or planes of a roof come together or when there is a penetration in the roof.
◆**WWW**◆

Flashing Valleys

Where two sections of sloped roof come together, there is good chance for water penetration because of the large volume of water that is directed into a small channel. Flowing water will attempt to continue on a path even when it faces an obstacle. Water flowing down a steep roof will not simply flow into the valley, but will try to run up into the opposing roof section. Leaks can occur here because the water can flow up under the opposing shingles. Remember, shingles and tiles only work when water runs over top of them because they work by shedding the water. Valley flashing works by tucking under the shingles on either side of the valley so that any water that gets under the shingles flows back to the flashing and back down the valley.

Flashing Penetrations
Penetrations will have to be made through the roof for things like plumbing vent pipes and roof vents. This can pose a tricky flashing problem. If a vent is intended to work with a shingled roof, a flange should surround the bottom of the vent. This flange integrates with the shingles by tucking under the shingles above and to the sides and over the shingles below. When water flows down the roof the flange acts as a shingle keeping water from entering the roof.

Ice Dams (Cold Climates)
An ice dam is an ice formation at the end of a roof that prevents water from draining properly. When the water cannot flow over the shingles and off the roof, it backs up under the shingle, causing water damage to the roof sheathing, trusses, and possibly the walls and ceiling of the house.

Ice dams form in these conditions:

- snow or ice on the roof
- outside temperature below freezing
- some portion of the upper roof above freezing
- some portion of the lower roof below freezing

When you see icicles forming on the edge of a roof, you are seeing an ice dam forming. What is happening is that snow is melting in an upper portion of the roof and the resulting water is flowing down the roof until it hits an area of the roof below where the temperature is below freezing. When the water hits this area, it freezes and creates a dam. Then, as more water flows down the roof, it backs up at the dam. When the water backs up under the closest shingles, it enters the roof and causes water damage inside the house.

If it's below freezing outside, why is snow melting on my roof?

The main reason for roof snowmelt on a new home (other than the sun) is heat loss from the home's interior. This can be caused by improperly insulated ceilings, recessed lights, complicated roof designs (especially second floor vaulted areas), and heat ducts in the attic.

So, how will I know?

You will know if your house has a problem if you see snow on your roof melting at different rates or you see large icicles forming on the end of your roof. From the inside of the home, check for water staining where ceilings and walls intersect. In the attic, try to correlate the snow melt with a heat source- (i.e., can light, chimney, heat duct), but also check for signs of moisture under roof sheathing, on trusses or insulation.

Leaky Basements

Moisture in a basement of a new home can pose a number of problems. Besides making the basement less useable, the moisture can feed mold growth on everything in your basement from your first-floor joists to items simply stored down there. There is no shortage of moisture sources for a new basement:

- concrete curing: in the first couple of years, thousands of pounds of moisture will be expelled from the new concrete used to form your basement.
- sump well or crock: if water sits in an uncovered sump well it will evaporate into the air in your basement.
- exterior bulk water: even if you have proper drainage around your house, water will still soak into the ground. That water needs to be easily handled by the perimeter drainage system or drain tile and the sump pump.

A dehumidifier that discharges into a floor drain (not into the pan that is supplied with the unit) is a must in a new basement.

Water in Crawl Spaces

Moisture in crawl spaces can cause problems similar to those in basements. Standing water can feed mold growth and encourage termites and insects. If the level of the ground inside the crawl space is much lower than the grade outside, moisture can be forced through the crawl space walls. Inside perimeter drains can be installed to draw moisture to the outside.

Hidden Plumbing Leaks

Plumbing leaks can be caused by a number factors: poor soldering or gluing of pipes, pipe deterioration, damage from other contractors such as carpenters or dry-wallers. Builders and subcontractors should share the blame when a pipe is damaged by a nail or screw. For example, builders should mark the location on the floor of plumbing runs hidden behind walls so that subcontractors don't drive nails or screws through hidden pipes. Also, subcontractors such as trim carpenters should at least make an attempt to find a stud before firing their nail gun like a machine gun.

In performing restorations on newer homes I have seen a number of plumbing pipes with nails or screws driven through them. For the most part, the leaks went undetected because the nails or screws partially plugged the hole they made. The damage from supply pipes (hot and cold lines) is usually more noticeable and therefore easier to catch early on because these pipes are under pressure. Because waste lines are not under pressure, the likelihood of finding a leak without opening up a wall is less than with a supply pipe.

Damage to waste lines can create a small intermittent source of moisture to feed mold and mildew growth inside the wall cavity. The flush of a toilet can produce a small amount of water through a tiny nail hole in a waste pipe. Ongoing use of that toilet can lead to a buildup of moisture and hidden damage in the wall cavity. You can sometimes find these small leaks by walking around the perimeter of a room with your shoes off. Before you do this, though, make sure the water is on and all of the fixtures (faucets, showers) have been run and all of the toilets have been flushed several times. If the room is carpeted, you may be able to feel a moist area and have the builder find the leak.

In building a new house, it will be hard to avert the dreaded plumbing leak, but the repair needs to be handled carefully. When the leak saturates drywall or flooring, the wet material either needs to be dried completely or removed. If a wall, floor, or ceiling is sealed up before it dries, the likelihood is high for mold and mildew growth. If mold growth occurs, the affected area needs to be treated with a bleach solution and then thoroughly dried.

Vapor

Moisture vapor can be just as damaging to a new home as bulk water. Moisture vapor inside the house generated from cooking, cleaning, and even breathing can produce large amounts of moisture. The average family of four can produce 15 or more pints of water per day just from daily activities. In a new home, moisture-laden products drying and curing in your home are sources of additional wetness. Lumber products are kiln dried but may still release half of their post-kiln moisture content after installation. Curing concrete in a new home, especially one with poured concrete walls and floors, will release one to two thousand pounds of moisture in the first several years of a new home's life. And you thought you just had a problem from your spouse taking long showers!

Before the days of vapor barriers, heavy insulation, humidifiers, and central air conditioning, interior moisture would exit the home through drafty windows, doors, and walls. Today, if a new home is not properly ventilated, that moisture lingers. That is why it is critical to:

- turn on the bath or shower exhaust fan while the bath or shower are in use and leave the fan on for 15 to 20 minutes afterward
- use the kitchen range vent when cooking and make sure the fan exhausts to the outside and does not simply recirculate into the kitchen
- make sure that all exhaust fans vent to the outside, not to the attic or to the basement
- use heavy-gauge plastic film to cover exposed earth in a crawl space
- use a dehumidifier to help control the moisture evaporating from the curing concrete in the basement of a newer home

Vapor and Wall Cavities
Two extremes in temperature exerting pressure on a house increase the chance of moisture in the air condensing on cool surfaces. The principle is pretty simple. Just think of an ice-cold glass of water on a hot day. When warm, moist air comes in contact with the cold surface of the glass, water condenses on the outside of the glass. The same is true for you home. If you have a wall being cooled from the inside by an air conditioner on a hot day, there is a chance for condensation if warm moist air comes in contact with a cold surface. Ideally, insulation and vapor barriers are integrated into the wall system to prevent condensation, but in mixed climates where the summers are brutally hot and the winters frigid, it is difficult to build an energy efficient wall that works well.

Moisture problems affect homes differently in different areas of the country. Discuss moisture problems with your architect and have him or her find out how your builder deals with them.

Appendix B: Concrete

Concrete on the home site has many uses. From flatwork such as patios and walkways to vertical applications such as basement and retaining walls, concrete is the preferred material.

Concrete is a mixture of Portland cement, aggregate, sand, and water. With such a simple mix, it would seem there couldn't be much to mess up. But it's how this simple mixture is treated that determines the durability, strength, and appearance of the final product.

Before discussing anything about concrete, though, it is important to remember one thing: all concrete cracks! That is the nature of concrete and a result of the curing of the concrete and the load to which it is subjected. There hasn't been a walk-through I have performed with a homeowner where they haven't raised concerns about nonstructural cracking in a wall, driveway, sidewalk, patio, or garage. Minor hairline cracks are one thing, but cracking caused by poor sub-grade preparation (preparing the material below), bad mix of concrete ingredients, poor finishing, or freeze-thaw cycles is unacceptable.

Preparation
Think of concrete slabs as ice on a frozen lake -- if the ice is thick enough and in contact with water below, the ice can support the weight of a house. But if cracks cut across the ice or create thin spots, watch out! The same is true for concrete slabs. It is important that concrete slabs (such as garage floors) be placed on a well-compacted bed of gravel, sand, or other fill material. If the material under the slab is not compacted or settled, voids

have a good chance of forming under the slab after the concrete has cured.

If a void develops under the slab nothing supports the slab above and more than likely a crack will develop when a load is applied to the area. Using the frozen lake analogy, you could fall through the ice!

For foundations, sub-grade material must be not only compacted, but also very stable. Foundations typically settle because of the concentrated force placed on the ground below. For example, a garage floor's weight is spread over a larger area than the foundation footer that may only be a few feet wide. If settling of the entire house takes place minimally and uniformly, there is not much problem. But if one part of the structure settles more than the other, one part of the home may begin to pull away from the other.

The amount of settling that takes place depends on the soil type and compaction. If a foundation and basement are poured on well-compacted dense soil, there is less chance of settling. The exception occurs during a drought in an area with heavy clay soil. Problems arise when the clay dehydrates and shrinks because there is so little rain for several months. As the usually stable clay contracts, structures began to settle more than usual. The good thing is that the settling can be uniform if the dehydration rate of the clay is uniform.

When concrete is poured over an area that was previously excavated and then filled, such as a garage, patio, or stoop, it is important that the fill material has a chance to settle and then is further compacted before the slab is poured.

Garages

When a poured concrete foundation is constructed, an area is excavated to allow for the installation of footers and the foundation wall itself. After the walls cure, the area is backfilled. This backfill material *always* settles unless it is compacted. If the material is on the outside of a wall, it is not that big of a problem because more soil is placed over it as fill-in. The problem occurs when concrete is poured over this unsettled area. Such is the case with a garage floor. If the area under the garage floor is not backfilled with an easily compacted material such as gravel, then a great deal of settling can take place under the slab, resulting in a dropped garage floor.

Again, if this garage drops minimally and uniformly, there is not much of a problem. But if voids develop under the slab, the slab can crack when a load is applied (such as a car).

Sidewalks

Another trademark of a builder that doesn't understand settling of backfilled material is the sunken driveway, walkway, or porch. This settling usually takes place because of poor backfilling of the foundation wall or trench from underground utilities. You now know about backfilling garages and basements, and the same theory applies to trenches. When underground utilities such as electricity, gas, and water are installed, a trench is dug. The deeper this trench is, the greater the chance of settling. There are ways to prevent settling over trenches, though. The natural way is simply waiting! Over time, the clumps of earth that were dumped back into the trench will compact under their own weight and more fill can be placed over it. Another trick of the trade is to introduce water to the fill, which accelerates the settling. The preferred method is to use sand or gravel to backfill a trench. Sand and gravel have fewer air pockets than clumps of soil, especially clay or frozen soil, so fewer voids have to be filled. If the builder pours a walkway over an uncompacted trench, the soil will settle and a void will develop under the slab, leaving it unsupported.

Pouring

The concrete mixture is delivered to the job premixed in a concrete truck. The truck is designed to prevent separating or hardening of the materials by keeping the mixture in motion. A limited time frame exists during which the mixture will remain "good." A driver can "lose" a load of concrete by waiting too long to pour it.

Different applications of concrete have different ideal consistencies. In general, the less runny the mixture is as it leaves the chute of the concrete truck, the stronger the finished product will be. One of the most common measures of a concrete mixture is the "slump test." In reality, this test is usually performed in commercial applications (as opposed to residential) where there is set specifications for the concrete because of the load the concrete will experience. More than likely, a semi or tractor-trailer won't drive across your patio and your house won't be 30 stories high! Nevertheless, it is important that a high-quality mixture is used for any application. The slump test is one way to verify the quality of the mixture.

To conduct a slump test, fresh concrete is poured into a 12" cone that looks like a construction warning cone. The cone is then inverted and removed from the wet mixture. The distance it has settled from the top of the cone is measured.

The more the cone holds its shape, the stronger the concrete is said to be. However, a good balance between workability and strength is desirable. A good slump rating would be about a "four" for residential applications. A "four-slump" rating means that in a standard cone test, the top of the mixture would drop four inches from the top of the cone.

Finishing

The finishing of the concrete is a real art form. If you don't think so, try pouring and finishing a basement slab or a long driveway sometime!

As the concrete is poured into a formed area, it is distributed evenly across the compacted fill. The depth of the concrete varies depending on the application, but the rule of thumb in residential applications is four inches thick for slabs (basements, garages, driveways, and walkways).

The concrete mix is pushed and pulled into a uniform thickness by special tools that look like rakes with closed tines. If the mixture has the recommended "four" slump, it takes some muscle to distribute the mixture. If the slump is high, it is much easier to work with because the mix would almost be self-leveling. But remember, the "runnier" the mixture, the weaker the final product.

The slab is then "bull-floated," which puts a first semi-smooth finish on the slab. This first pass allows the slab to "bleed," meaning the water from the mixture bleeds to the surface right after it is poured. The water that rises to the top *must* be allowed to evaporate before the surface is troweled. This step in the finishing process is critical to assuring consistent water content throughout the slab. If the top of the slab has a higher slump because of water content, the top of the slab will be weaker.

It is tempting for the finisher to trowel the surface smooth while it is bleeding because the higher water content at the surface makes it much easier to work with. But remember, too much water means the strength of the concrete is diminished.

The bleed time varies depending on the conditions. In warm and windy conditions, the water that rises to the top during bleeding evaporates fairly quickly, just like a very shallow puddle on a warm windy day.

After the bleeding and evaporation take place, the slab is ready for the finish. The finish varies depending on the applications, but typically, a basement and garage will have a smooth finish and driveways and walkways will have a broom finish to increase traction.

Exposed Aggregate
An attractive alternative to the standard gray concrete slab is the exposed aggregate finish. In this application the proportion of aggregate stones in the mixture is increased and the surface of the slab is weakened with chemical retarders. After the slab has sat for a day to set up, the weakened surface is sprayed off, exposing the stone in the mixture. This finish requires a skilled hand, because you only want to weaken the surface of the slab, not the entire slab.

Cold Weather Precautions
Pouring concrete in cold conditions poses a serious challenge. Concrete mixtures can be sent from the plant with hot water or chemical additives that speed up the curing process, but this may be less than ideal. Remember, concrete cures as the water evaporates from the mixture. If it's freezing out, there won't be a lot of evaporatin' goin' on!

First of all, concrete cannot be poured on frozen ground. If you pour a warm mixture of concrete on a frozen surface, the warm mixture will melt the frozen ground, releasing more water into the mixture and resulting in a weaker concrete. Also, frozen ground may "heave" and then return to its original form when it thaws. This instability makes for a poor surface to support the concrete.

As far as finishing goes, it is nearly impossible to get a good finish on concrete in conditions below freezing. It is not recommended that concrete be poured in conditions below 32° Fahrenheit unless the area can be heated. If the concrete will be exposed to freezing temperatures soon after it is finished, special blankets can be applied over the slab to hold in the heat.

Reinforcing
Concrete slabs need a little help "holding it all together." The addition of steel reinforcement bars (re-bar) provides that support. As I mentioned at the beginning of this section, it's a fact that concrete cracks. Rebar prevents those cracks from becoming too large. Re-bar can also be used to "tie" together different pieces of concrete. For example, re-bar is often used to "tie" together a porch stoop to the walkway and the garage slab to the poured walls on top of it.

When you look at re-bar you see ribs in the steel. It is this ribbing that binds the steel to the concrete. Think about a Popsicle on a stick. If you bite off half of the frozen Popsicle, it slides off the stick. But if that stick was ribbed or notched, the frozen treat would have a tough time sliding off of the stick. The same is true for concrete. When the slab cracks, it is the ribs in the steel that keep it from separating.

It is important that the rebar actually be embedded in the middle of the concrete. The re-bar should not just lie on the ground with the concrete poured on top of it. If the re-bar just sits on the bottom of the slab, it serves no structural purpose.

Re-bar is also important in poured concrete walls. Its added strength keeps small cracks from becoming big problems.

Cracking and Joints

Yes, concrete cracks, but an attempt should be made to anticipate where the cracks will occur by placing control joints (gaps between concrete sections) in the concrete. Control joints are dug into the wet concrete while the finish is put on, or cut in later with a concrete saw. You've seen the control joint before; they are the gaps that create the "blocks" in the sidewalk or driveway.

If the joint is put in at the finish stage, a notched trowel is used to dig a groove in the wet slab. This groove needs to be about an inch deep to ensure that the crack takes place there and not in a random location. Control joint spacing is determined by the width of the slab, but joints should never be placed more than twelve feet apart. On a sidewalk that is four feet wide, control joints should be placed every four feet.

Some concrete slabs need to be separate by design. Where slabs have been poured at different times and have different uses, a special material needs to keep the sections independent. In some areas such as where the concrete driveway meets the garage, an asphalt impregnated fibrous material (tar paper) is installed between the two materials before the pour to completely separate the slabs.

Crack Detective

Cracking will take place in slabs and poured concrete walls, but how do you know when a crack is compromising the strength or performance of the concrete?

Slabs

As mentioned before, concrete slabs need to be poured on a well-compacted base of granular soil, sand, or gravel. If settling takes place under the slab, the concrete will be left unsupported and has the potential to crack. Although you may not see what is taking place under a slab of cured concrete (unless there is severe erosion or settling), you can tell a settling crack from a shrinkage crack by the size of the crack. Typically, if the crack exceeds one-quarter inch in width or depth, it is said to be a symptom of a structural problem. The problem is not with the concrete, although that is what you see, but rather with the settling of the material under the slab.

Poured Walls
Structural cracking in poured concrete walls is indicated by a gap of greater than 1/8". Again, this type of cracking is more likely a symptom of pressure against the wall than it is from the concrete failing.

Spalling, Dusting, Scaling
The deterioration of the top layer of concrete can usually be attributed to a poor finish job or the introduction of a de-icer (like road salt) or fertilizer that contains ammonia nitrate or ammonia sulfate.

As mentioned earlier, not allowing the concrete mix to bleed before finishing creates higher moisture content in the top layer of the slab. When this weakened layer is exposed to the freeze/thaw cycle or a heavy load such as car traffic, the surface can pop and expose the aggregate (gravel) in the slab. Usually the damage to the top layer is cosmetic and does not affect the overall strength of the slab. If, however, the entire mix had a higher moisture content when poured (high slump) the integrity of the slab has been jeopardized.

Because concrete, like brick and mortar, is porous, it absorbs water and is thus susceptible to the damaging effects of freeze and thaw cycles. If excessive moisture is present in the concrete when the temperature drops below freezing, the water can turn to ice and cause damage to the surface of the slab. When de-icing agents such as salt are used, the number of freeze-thaw cycles increases, adding more stress to the concrete. In cooler climates, concrete should be sealed (usually done by the homeowner) before winter to decrease the amount of moisture that the slab can absorb.

Exterior concrete should be cared for in a similar manner to asphalt by sealing the surface and limiting the load. To help prevent the absorption of moisture, concrete should be sealed with a clear concrete sealer. You should also keep that moving truck in the street; remember: it's a driveway, not a roadway.

Appendix C: Plumbing

The plumbing system in your new home should go unnoticed. You should be able to take showers and have plenty of hot water, never have a leaky faucet or a toilet that overflows. That is what *should* happen, but we know that it is not always the case. There is always the chance your water heater will only handle a few showers, a leaky faucet will keep you up at night, or an overflowed toilet will ruin your hardwood floors. So let's get smart about plumbing!

Your new home will most likely have a combination of copper, plastic, iron, and stainless steel pipes. Each serves a different purpose and can be used in different applications.

Copper
Copper piping has been the standard in many houses for the delivery of hot and cold water to fixtures (faucets, shower heads, etc.) for decades. Copper is a very durable material that, when installed properly, will offer a lifetime of worry-free use. Most installation-related problems with copper will be noticed very early in a home's life, while problems such as corrosion will not show up for years. ◆**WWW**◆

Copper pipe used in the United States is graded according to ASTM (American Society for Testing and Materials) guidelines. All copper should have a marking indicating its wall thickness. Copper grades for residential systems are K, L, and M, where K is stronger than L, and L is stronger than M. The common rating for residential water supply is type M.

Copper pipe is connected with solder joints. The copper joint is heated with a torch until it is hot enough to melt the solder into the joint, creating a strong, metallic bond. Failure in one of these joints will often be noticed as soon as the system is pressurized. The risk here is that the water supply is often not "turned on" until the fixtures are in place, one of the last things that happens in the construction of a house. Although it is not uncommon for a water leak to show up in a wall or ceiling after the water is turned on, the damage caused by a leak so late in the game can be terrible.

Small, persistent leaks can be even more damaging than a sudden burst pipe. In the case of a sudden burst, the damage is immediately apparent and can be repaired. In the case of a small persistent leak, moisture can slowly feed dangerous mold spores. A constant moisture source combined with the dark, fiber-rich conditions that exist inside wall cavities can spell disaster. ♦**WWW**♦

Benefits

- Copper's main benefit is its durability. As mentioned before, installed properly, copper will last a lifetime.
- Copper is fireproof so it will not feed a fire or allow it to travel to another part of a structure.
- Copper is bendable to a degree, allowing for a more forgiving installation.

Drawbacks

- Copper's main drawback vs. plastic is cost. Copper pipe, as well as the associated installation, is more expensive than plastic.
- Copper is connected using a torch, so there is a slight safety concern.

- Copper can break down when exposed to high acid levels that exist in some well water systems. Industry experts recommend a water conditioner to be used when water in domestic systems has a pH less than 6.8. Most city water systems have a pH of between 7 and 9 so the problem mostly affects homes not connected to municipal water.

Plastics

Even if you have copper tubing delivering hot and cold water in your new home, chances are good that plastic pipe serves as the drain, waste, and vent (DWV) conduit.

Plastic pipe falls into either the rigid or flexible category.

Rigid

Most rigid plastic is used for drain, waste, and vent applications. If you look under most sinks you will see a rigid white plastic used as the drain. During construction you will also see that same plastic used for toilet drains and for venting the waste lines to the roof.

Polyvinyl chloride (PVC) and chlorinated polyvinyl chloride (CPVC) are the two most common types of rigid plastic pipe. They are white or off white in color. PVC, the whiter of the two plastics, can only be used in wastewater applications and for venting because it is not designed for high temperatures. CPVC pipe, or Flow Guard Gold, as it is know by one of its brand names, is used to deliver both hot and cold water.

Rigid plastic pipes are connected using solvents (glues). The connections are much easier to make than copper fittings. ♦**WWW**♦

Benefits

- The biggest benefit of rigid plastic pipe is its cost and ease of installation. The pipe is easy to cut and connect, reducing labor costs.
- PVC and CPVC are chemically stable and are not affected by different pH levels.
- PVC and CPVC are also quieter than copper, have a smoother inner wall to reduce buildup of scale, and reduce the amount of pipe sweating.

Drawbacks

- The biggest drawback of plastic pipe is that its not as durable (at proper pH levels) as copper.
- CPVC manufacturers claim that the product will last a lifetime, but it has not been around for a lifetime to prove that claim.
- Plastic will melt and burn at much lower temperatures than copper.
- Rigid plastic pipe is not bendable, so in those tight places, more fittings may be needed.
- CPVC is not approved in all states for the supply of hot and cold water.

Flexible Plastic

Flexible plastic tubing, commonly known as PEX (cross-linked polyethylene) has been used for years in the mobile home industry as well as in the delivery of radiant heat through floors and baseboard radiators. PEX's ability to withstand the pressure and temperature of a radiant heating system increased its popularity for the delivery of domestic water. Because the product is not widely used nationwide, a limited number of plumbers are familiar with the product.

Benefits

- PEX is highly flexible and easy to install. Making runs is more like wiring a house than plumbing it.
- Because many fewer connections are used, the rate of flow is not reduced by a series of fittings.

Drawbacks

- PEX is not much cheaper than copper and is not widely used in the plumbing industry, so there is not much of a cost savings, certainly not over CPVC.
- PEX expands when exposed to heat (including hot water), so it will sag if not supported properly.

Waste Lines

Drains in your sinks and toilets work by gravity, with the help of air relief. The vents in the waste water system increase the flow of the wastewater through pipes. The vents act the same way as the holes you would find in a gasoline can used to fill your grass mower or chainsaw. Without the second hole to let air in, the gasoline would come out in "gulps." The toilet drain system is not different. Without an air vent pipe, your flush would occur in "gulps" as well. ♦**WWW**♦

Pressure

Two types of pressure are commonly exerted on a residential plumbing system that can limit its life. The first is the pressure that is developed by the creation of hot water called thermal pressure (as we know from cooking). If that pressure is not properly dissipated when created, damage can be caused to fixtures (faucets) throughout the system. Thermal pressure can be dissipated with the use of an expansion system, typically located close to the water heater in the hot water line. ♦**WWW**♦

The sudden closing of valves that are commonly found on dishwashers and washing machines causes the other type of pressure that is common in residential water systems. You have probably experienced "water hammer" if you have ever seen a wash machine change cycles or a shower turn off suddenly. Quickly closing of a valve causes pressure behind the valve, which in turn causes stress on pipes, fittings, and fixtures "upstream." Using a water hammer "arrestor" can prevent water hammer. ♦**WWW**♦

During walk-throughs, I always showed customers where the home's main water shut-off is located. I explain that, in case of a water leak, homeowners should immediately shut off the main water valve coming into the house. I always stress that the valve should be turned off slowly in order to prevent the damage that can occur from quickly stopping the pressure of water.

Fixtures
There will be several fixtures to choose from when it comes to making your selections for your new home.

Faucets
Selecting a quality faucet from a well-known manufacturer will give you years of trouble- free operation. If the builder states that a certain manufacturer's product will be used, make sure that is what is installed in your home. Again, you should have it in writing. The faucet will come with a warranty from the manufacturer. Make sure you get a copy of it and understand whether it covers only the operation of the fixture, or if it also covers the finish of the faucet (polished chrome, brass, gold, etc.).

Toilets

Since 1992, toilets sold in the United States have had to comply with a stricter standard of water usage. The law was intended to save water by reducing the amount of allowable water used per flush. Now that the "low flow" toilet has become the standard, consumers are increasingly registering complaints about the performance of some models. There are good low-flow toilets out on the market, but the question is, does your builder offer them?
♦WWW♦

Water Heaters

Water heaters are rated by their capacity not just for storage but also for recovery, or how quickly they can replace the hot water as it is used.

If natural gas is available, go with a gas water heater. A gas water heater has a quicker recovery time (the time it takes to heat the water in the tank) so a smaller tank is required. For a family of four, a 50-gallon tank is recommended.

Plumbing Pitfalls:

When it comes to plumbing, there are really only a few things that the untrained new homeowner can look for:

1. *Test caps left on.* In a typical plumbing system vents in the system allow sewer gas to escape and the waste water to drain. **♦WWW♦** Because the drain, waste, and vent system does not hold water all the time, it is hard to detect leaks. One way to test the system is to pressurize it. In order for this to happen, the system must be sealed, and that means temporarily capping off the vents on the roof. Plumbers have the tendency to forget to remove one or all of the caps on the roof. Maybe it's raining

when they come back to the house to check on the test. Maybe the plumber didn't see the cap on the other side of the roof. For whatever reason, caps get left on. Its OK if you catch it early on, but I have seen houses where a cap has been left on for almost three years! In cases of caps left on, the toilets perform as if they are perpetually clogged!

2. *Switched hot and cold lines.* This is something that should be checked in the walk-through. Don't let the builder leave the water heater unlit or turned off so you can't check for this. Check every fixture to make sure hot is hot and cold is cold.

3. *Clogged fixtures.* This can happen both on the interior and exterior of your home. Inside, especially with copper pipes, debris can flow through the system and get trapped by the screens in faucets. Outside, especially on brick homes, mortar and debris can clog the anti-siphon features on hose bibs.

4. *Nails through drain pipes.* Holes in supply lines are usually easy to spot because pressure always exists in the supply lines. Small holes in drain lines are harder to spot because the pipes are not under pressure. One way to spot small holes in drain lines is to operate every fixture during the walk-through: tubs, toilets, and sinks. The water will flow into the drains and possibly out of any holes in pipes. As you walk through the house, make sure you do so without your shoes on so that you can feel for any leaks along the perimeter of rooms.

5. *Not knowing where your main shut-off is.* Make sure your builder shows you the location of the main water shut-off for the whole house. If a pipe breaks, you need to be able to quickly shut off the water to prevent catastrophic damage.

Appendix D: Wood

Wood is the main component in most homes across the county. In a modern home, a wide variety of wood materials range from 2x4 studs to "composite" trim material (such as baseboards and door casings) made only of paper and glue. Many homeowners are dismayed that cheap modern versions of traditional wood have found their way into the entryways, mantels, and trim of their new house. Some new wood "composites" or "replacements" are good alternatives to traditional lumber while others are just cheap imitations. Let's take a look at some of the different uses for wood and wood alternatives in today's homes.

Framing

Most people are familiar with the 2x4 inch or 2x6 inch stud framed wall. The most common types of wood used by builders for studs are Southern Pine and Douglas Fir. The idea here is strength, not necessarily beauty, although they are usually related. Grades of lumber vary widely, depending on things such as the part of the tree the lumber came from as well as how many knots the lumber contains. Some builders pride themselves on using top grade lumber for studs while others use the minimal "stud grade" stock, figuring that studs will be unseen and provide no visible benefit to the homeowner. If the builder is not open about the quality of lumber they use, you can identify the grade of the lumber by visiting a home that is being framed. Lumber grades for studs can be found on a stamp on the lumber or the bundle that it was shipped with. A link to a chart of grades can be found on our site. ♦**WWW**♦

Moisture Content

When lumber is cut from a log, it is said to be "green" until it has dried. To speed up this drying process, lumber producers kiln dry their wood, but it will still dry further. When the lumber is delivered to the job site, its moisture content can be as high as 19 percent. When stud grade lumber is in a temperature-controlled environment like a finished house, its moisture content drops to around 8 percent. This reduction in moisture content can shrink a 2x4's horizontal measurement by one-eighth of an inch! This shrinking is normal, but if the studs can't reach their equilibrium moisture content (which will be dependent on the climate) before drywall is applied, problems will occur.

Most nail pops occur when drywall nails or screws securing a sheet of drywall to a stud or ceiling move as a result of a force applied by the shrinking or bowing of lumber. If the stud behind the drywall does not have stable moisture content, any screw or nail secured to it will move as the stud shrinks and swells. The stud's movement causes the drywall compound or "mud" and paint to "pop," which exposes the nail or screw head.

Floor Joists

Floor joists run the length of the floor and support the subfloor above. The floor joists can be made of dimensional lumber (such as 2x8's or 2x10's) or with engineered lumber. Dimensional lumber, whether a 2x4 stud or a 2x10 floor joist, will be imperfect. The shrinking, swelling, twisting, and bowing that take place are natural. The alternative is to use an engineered lumber product.

Engineered lumber

Lumber producers have created products that combine wood products with glues and laminates that correct problems inherent in solid sawed lumber. Engineered lumber resists warping and shrinking because it is a manufactured product. Using the same thinking that produced plywood, engineered wood products are usually lighter and stronger than their sawed lumber counterparts.

Glued laminated timber (Glulam), Laminated Veneer Lumber (LVL) Paralam Beams

In certain applications, such as over garage door openings, beams span a large area and need to be strong and stable. If the beam is sawed from a single log, the chance is pretty good that the beam will not hold its original shape. The alternative is an engineered beam that takes advantage of the strength and stability of laminating wood. Images and uses of each can be found on our Web site. ♦**WWW**♦

Plywood and Oriented Strand Board (OSB)

Subfloors, roof sheathing, and exterior wall sheathing are usually made of either plywood or Oriented Strand Board.

Plywood

Plywood is made by laminating thin wood veneers. The veneers are placed in alternating patterns so that any shrinkage in the wood is minimized. When nailed to floor joists, studs, or trusses, a strong sturdy surface is created.

OSB

A less expensive and structurally weaker alternative to plywood is Oriented Strand Board or OSB. OSB is made by gluing together small wafers of wood that are oriented in a way to maximize strength and minimize shrinkage. Because the wafers are not as large as the wood veneers used in plywood, OSB tends not to be as strong as plywood when used as a roof sheathing or subfloor. OSB does have considerable strength to prevent racking (to prevent a wall from collapsing) and is therefore well suited for exterior sheathing or as part of engineered floor joists such as "wood I-beams."

Interior trim products

Real Solid Wood
More and more, builders are using wood alternatives for interior trim because buyers in most price ranges do not see the value in using a real wood product that will simply be painted over. Of course, if your home will have stained wood trim, the only option is to use real wood, expensive as it may be.

Finger-jointed
Long, solid wood pieces of trim such as baseboard and chair rail are expensive. An alternative to continuous real wood trim is finger-jointed trims. Finger-jointed trim uses shorter pieces of lumber joined together with a finger-joint and glue to make a single long piece of trim.

MDF
Medium density fiberboard uses wood byproducts that are glued together and formed to create different shapes. The profile of the trim mimics that of real wood products and is available in almost all of the same applications such as baseboard and crown molding. The drawback is that the material cannot be sanded (it would be like sanding cardboard) and can swell if it gets wet. The benefits are that the material is much more flexible than real wood, is difficult to mar or dent, and is delivered with a flawless surface.

Exterior Trim

Wood composites and alternatives are replacing real wood for interior and exterior trim. Trim used around windows and doors or for siding in many new homes is more than likely not real wood. This can be good or bad depending on the application and the material. Wood composites can be mixtures of wood fiber and cements or resins. "Paper and glue" products must be installed and maintained with care because they can absorb water quite easily, but are preferred by builders because of the cost. A much more durable alternative is plastic. Plastic trim is very moisture resistant and can be molded to look like expensive millwork. Since the use of wood alternatives varies across the country, check out the link on our Web site for a listing of all products and installation and maintenance suggestions.

State-by-state Contact Information for Attorney General

State	Phone Number	Web Site
Alabama	334-242-7300	http://www.ago.state.al.us/
Alaska	907-465-3600	http://www.law.state.ak.us/
Arizona	800-352-8431	http://www.ag.state.az.us/
Arkansas	501-682-2007	http://www.ag.state.ar.us/
California	800-952-5225	http://caag.state.ca.us/
Colorado	800-332-2071	http://www.ago.state.co.us/
Connecticut	860-808-5318	http://www.cslnet.ctstateu.edu/attygenl/
Delaware	302-577-8300	http://www.state.de.us/attgen/index.htm
Florida	904-487-1963	http://legal.firn.edu/
Georgia	404-656-3300	http://www.georgianet.org/ago/
Hawaii	808-586-1282	http://www.hawaii.gov/ag/
Idaho	208-334-2424	http://www2.state.id.us/ag/index.html
Illinois	800-243-0618	http://www.ag.state.il.us/
Indiana	800-382-5516	http://www.state.in.us/attorneygeneral/
Iowa	515-281-6771	http://www.state.ia.us/government/ag/index.html

Kansas	785-296-2215	http://www.ink.org/public/ksag/
Kentucky	502-696-5389	http://www.law.state.ky.us/
Louisiana	504-342-7013	http://www.ag.state.la.us/
Maine	207-626-8849	http://www.state.me.us/ag/homepage.htm
Maryland	410-528-8662	http://www.oag.state.md.us/
Massachusetts	617-727-8400	http://www.ago.state.ma.us/condefault.asp
Michigan	877-765-8388	http://www.ag.state.mi.us/
Minnesota	800-657-3787	http://www.ag.state.mn.us/
Mississippi	800-281-4418	http://www.ago.state.ms.us/
Missouri	573-751-3321	http://www.ago.state.mo.us/index.htm
Montana	406-444-2026	http://www.doj.state.mt.us/ago/index.htm
Nebraska	402-471-2682	http://www.nol.org/home/ago/
Nevada	800-266-8688	http://ag.state.nv.us/
New Hampshire	603-271-3641	http://www.state.nh.us/nhdoj/index.html
New Jersey	609-292-4925	http://www.state.nj.us/lps/oag.html
New Mexico	800-678-1508	http://www.ago.state.nm.us/
New York	800-771-7755	http://www.oag.state.ny.us/
North Carolina	919-716-6000	http://www.jus.state.nc.us/
North Dakota	800-472-2600	http://www.ag.state.nd.us/

Ohio	800-282-0515	http://www.ag.state.oh.us/default.htm
Oklahoma	405-521-3921	http://www.oag.state.ok.us/oagweb.nsf
Oregon	877-877-9392	http://www.doj.state.or.us/
Pennsylvania	800-441-2555	http://www.attorneygeneral.gov/
Rhode Island	800-852-7776	http://www.riag.state.ri.us/
South Carolina	803-734-3970	http://www.scattorneygeneral.org/
South Dakota	800-300-1986	http://www.state.sd.us/attorney/attorney.html
Tennessee	615-741-3491	http://www.attorneygeneral.state.tn.us/
Texas	512-463-2191	http://www.oag.state.tx.us/
Utah	801-538-1326	http://www.attygen.state.ut.us/
Vermont	800-649-2424	http://www.state.vt.us/atg/
Virginia	804-786-2071	http://www.oag.state.va.us/
Washington	800-551-4636	http://www.wa.gov/ago/
West Virginia	800-368-8808	http://www.state.wv.us/wvag/
Wisconsin	608-224-4960	http://www.doj.state.wi.us/
Wyoming	307-777-7841	http://attorneygeneral.state.wy.us/

Contacts:

Real Estate Attorney

Name: _____
Address:_____
Phone: _____

Checklist:
☐ Purchase Agreement/ Contract
☐ Warranty
☐ Addendums
☐ Plot Plan
☐ HOA Documents
☐ CCR

Inspector

Name: _____
Address: _____
Phone: _____

Checklist:
☐ Exact House Plan
☐ Plot Plan
☐ Specification Sheet
☐ Schedule

Comparable Checklist

Use this checklist when comparing homes from different builders as described in Chapters Five and Six.

___ Location

___ Schools

___ Neighborhood
    Amenities

___ Income Tax

___ Warranty

___ Builder Reputation

___ Cost of
    Options/Upgrades

___ Lot Size/Quality

___ Mortgage Incentives

___ Exterior Features

___ Siding

___ Windows

___ Driveway

___ Patio

___ Exterior Lighting

___ Exterior Doors

___ Interior Features

___ Flooring
    Grade/Allowance

___ Lighting/Allowance

___ Interior Doors

___ Door Hardware

___ Wall/Ceiling Finish

___ HVAC size

___ Water Heater Size

___ Plumbing Fixtures

___ Garage Size

___ Front/Side Entry

___ Room Sizes

___ Kitchen Features

___ Appliance Quality

___ Cabinet Features

___ Master Bedroom

___ Tub/ Shower

___ Closets

___ Storage

Index:

Have You Been HADD?
Homeowners Against Deficient Dwellings (HADD)

A consumer protection group for homeowners and home buyers.

www.HADD.com

This Gift Certificate entitles you to receive $20 off the purchase of any carpet or area rug at KidCarpet.com

Please go to: **http://www.kidcarpet.com** to select a rug.

Then call 1-888-308-4884 to make your purchase and redeem your coupon. Please use coupon code HBP1 when ordering

www.kidcarpet.com

Quick Order Page

⇒**Telephone Orders:** Call (888)-578-0766 Toll Free
Visa, MasterCard, American Express Accepted

⇒**Online Orders:** www.HomeBuildingPitfalls.com

⇒**Postal Orders:**   New Community Press
                        HBP Order
                        2692 Madison Road N-1 #263
                        Cincinnati, Ohio 45208

Number of Books: _____ @ $24.95 = $ _____

Name: _____

Address: _____

City: _____ State:_____ Zip: _____

Telephone: (_____) _____

e-mail address:_____

Sales Tax: Ohio residents please include State sales tax.
Price includes shipping within the Continental U.S.

Payment: ☐ Check ☐ Visa ☐ MasterCard ☐ AMEX

Card Number: _____
Name on Card: _____ Exp. Date: _____

HomeBuilding
PITFALLS

www.HomeBuildingPitfalls.com